The Lace Ghetto

The Lace Ghetto

Maxine Nunes and Deanna White

New Woman series: 3

General Editor: Adrienne Clarkson

new press / Toronto / 1972

Design / Peter Maher

ISBN cloth 0-88770-049-7
     paper 0-88770-075-6

new press
Order department
553 Richmond Street West
Toronto 133, Ontario

Manufactured in Canada by The Hunter Rose Company

To our mothers

To our fathers

With special love to:
   Eurico and Howard
And with special thanks to:
   Marilyn Beker, Joan Bodger, Sherrill Cheda, Ingrid
   Cook, Nell Hall-Humpherson, Kimberly, Mary Norton,
   Dodi Robb, Cynthia Scott, Judy Stoffman, Terry
   Thompson, Julie Wierzbicki, and the people of the
   women's movement

Thanks also to the following:
The CBC for permitting us to reprint the following material
from our "Women Now" television series: interviews
with suffragettes Nell Hall-Humpherson and Therese
Casgrain; with teenagers and Ron Lambert in Chapter 3,
"Socialization"; with the women in Chapter 8, "Consciousness
Raising"; with the men in Chapter 9, "Equal to What?";
with Marni Grobba, Heather Petrie, and Maryonn Kantaroff
in Chapter 4, "Fashion".

Helen Hutchinson who conducted the television interviews
with Nell Hall-Humpherson, Therese Casgrain, the teenagers,
the executives and the working men.

Danny Finkleman who interviewed the men in women's
liberation for "Equal to What".

Ain Soodor for the title Lace Ghetto.

The CBC Reference Library (Rose Allen, Pat Cooke, Ursula
Gojkovic, Michele Howland, Shirley McClellan, Elvira Selmys,
Blanche Smith, Cathy Spero).

The Toronto Public Library.

For permission to use copyrighted material grateful
acknowledgement is made to the following authors and
publishers:

Bernard Geis Associates for excerpts from How to Get A
Teen-Age Boy and What to Do with Him When You Get Him
© 1969 by Ellen Peck and from The Baby Trap © 1971 by
Ellen Peck.

Granada Publishing Limited for excerpts from The Female
Eunuch by Germaine Greer.

Laura Jones for excerpt from her article "Childbirth as
Ceremony" (Guerilla, #17). Reprinted by permission of
Guerilla, © 1971.

Alfred A. Knopf, Inc. for excerpts from The Second Sex by
Simone de Beauvoir.

Ann Landers for excerpt from her column (Toronto Star).
Reprinted by permission of Publishers-Hall Syndicate.

Alan Lorber for excerpt from the "Groupies". Reprinted with
permission. © 1969 Alan Lorber Productions, Inc. All rights
reserved.

Maclean's Magazine for excerpt "Woman Less Truthful Than
Man" (Maclean's, June 1913).

William Morrow and Company, Inc. for excerpts from The
Dialectic of Sex by Shulamith Firestone.

Platt & Munk Publishers for excerpt from Our Favorite Things
by James Kruss, illustrated by Edith Witt. © 1969 by Platt
and Munk Publishers. © 1968 by BOJE-Verlag, Stuttgart
(Was Kleine Kinder Gerne Mogen).

Windmill Books/Simon and Schuster for excerpts from
I'm Glad I'm a Boy! I'm Glad I'm a Girl by Whitney Darrow.

Frank Zappa Music, Inc. for excerpt from the song "Plastic
People". © 1969 Frank Zappa Music Inc.

Every reasonable effort has been made to ascertain
copyright. If we have unwittingly infringed copyright in any
excerpt, picture or photograph reproduced in this book, we
tender our sincerest apologies and will be glad of the
opportunity, upon being satisfied as to the owner's title,
to pay an appropriate fee as if we had been able to obtain
prior permission.

Contents

1 Women Through the Eyes of Others / *1*

2 This Mad, Wicked Folly of Women's Rights
  Or   How We Won the Vote / *11*

3 Socialization / *37*

4 Fashion / *57*

5 Sexuality / *69*

6 Marriage / *93*

7 Motherhood / *107*

8 Consciousness Raising / *131*

9 Equal to What? / *141*

10 Postscript / *153*

Women through the eyes of others

Many of the great male writers and philosophers of our culture, whose task it is to interpret the human condition, have taken it upon themselves to define woman. But woman herself has not yet succeeded in defining her own identity. Even in this relatively enlightened century, the human condition continues to be considered as something quite apart from the female condition.

The attitudes of the sages quoted in this chapter have long been familiar to us. The astounding thing is that, until the current feminist explosion, women could read them without balking, without, perhaps, even permitting an underlying anger to surface. Through some tricky mental juggling we were able to separate "woman", as described by men, from "myself"— a female, assuredly, but not one of "those women".

In the next few pages we'll take a brief historical look at these attitudes towards women, which have served to define for us what we are, what we should be, what we cannot be. Later in this book, the damage done to us as individuals by sexual stereotyping will be dealt with in greater depth, by comparing the myths of female existence to the realities as described by women, as well as some men, who spoke to us about their lives.

But first we'll present the images of woman from as far back as the Bible (we were created as an afterthought to help out around the garden and subsequently have borne the burden of blame for having mankind expelled from paradise) to the portrayal of the female in today's mass media. By isolating those influences that have formed and motivated our behaviour (without our fully conscious knowledge), we will be able to see ourselves, and the world, through our own eyes and not through the eyes of others—the first step for anyone in reaching towards freedom.

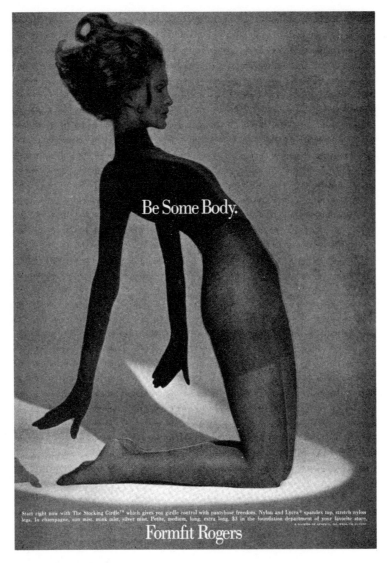

Woman's body is the woman.

Ambrose Bierce

To be beautiful is enough. If a woman can do that who shall demand more from her. You don't want a rose to sing.

William Makepeace Thackeray

I have created a playground for men's hands.

I, Armando Ghedini, adore women. I have created a wig for other men who adore women, too.

My Tenderly wig. It is wash and wear. It comes in many colors.

Men will soon make it famous among women. Because I have designed it with a wispy front, that can be combed any which way, for men to tousle. And with a long nape, for them to smooth around the swanlike neck of some breathtakingly feminine creature.

Men become inspired and impetuous when they are near women who wear the Tenderly.

That is why women are so grateful to me.

Be grateful for Ghedini.

North American Fashions, Inc., New York, San Francisco, Dallas, Hong Kong

When we accept this view of ourselves, we see only our reflection mirrored by another. In magazine ads, our eyes seem to look neither inward nor outward.

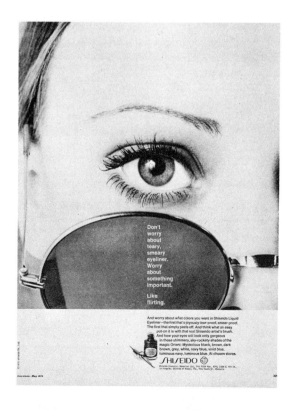

Our efforts to pour ourselves into whatever is the current mold of female beauty are often ludicrous. The whole exercise reached its nadir with the iron corsets of the last century, although we're still squeezing ourselves into forms that do not fit us. So much of our life's identity hinges on our image that it's not uncommon to see a seventy-year-old woman all powdered and rouged, crowned with a head of dyed blonde hair.

But despite all our efforts to please men—basing our identities on male approval—their opinion of us has historically been most unflattering.

The female is a female by virtue of a certain lack of qualities. We should regard the female as afflicted with a natural defectiveness.

Aristotle

Woman was made to yield to man and put up with his injustice.

Jean-Jacques Rousseau

In the East women religiously conceal that they have faces, in the West that they have legs. In both cases they make it evident that they have but little brains.

Henry David Thoreau

Woman is the lesser man.

Alfred Lord Tennyson

A man who has depth . . . can only think orientally about women. He must comprehend women as a possession, a property that can be closed off, as something predestined for service and thereby fulfilling its nature.

Friedrich Nietzsche

A New Approach that Works:

how to get & hold a woman

Generically, basically, woman "feels" while men "think." With women you had better adjust your thinking in terms of feelings.

"You have made a great contribution. . . . It is excellent. Dr. Cleo Dawson, psychoanalyst & lecturer.

Feelings, moods, and attitude (yours and hers) rule a woman, not facts, reason, nor logic. A man can start or stop any feeling (therefore, action) in no time at all.

"It presents an important subject in a new, explicit, and rewarding way." Dr. A. D. T.

The acquisition of knowledge or responsibilities does not lessen women's need for support, guidance, and control. Quite the contrary. Upbringing, mama, examples, T.V., radio, etc., do not suffice . . . she needs you. Woman acts solely on directives . . . so these had better be yours.

"Your book is fabulous . . . my marriage was never happier." Dr. R. G.

All women avoid, resist, repulse and object . . . but not because it's you. Why ask women when they only need to be told? Why ask women when they hope to be taken?

"I find it extremely informative, and very hard to believe that you don't know my wife personally." Dr. B. T. A.

"It has made my marriage jump up a few degrees." A. A. D.
"I know women but this volume is the graduate course." E. von B.
"I'm using your ways to get my family back together again." C. F.

". . . as a psychiatrist of 20 years experience and . . . lecturer in psychiatry . . . I heartily endorse your philosophy . . ."

J. M., M.D., F.A.P.A.

(No C.O.D.) (Full refund guaranteed if book is returned in 10 days)
Hardcover $10.00. Sold direct only. *Postage and all prepaid.*

G. C. PAYETTE
Marriage Counselor
1825 Rockland Road, Dept. C, Montreal 304, Canada

This view of woman as inferior and subservient gains legitimacy from the earliest and most sacred writings of civilization.

Let the woman learn in silence with all subjection. Suffer not a woman to teach, nor to usurp authority over the man, but to be in silence. . . . And if they will learn anything, let them ask their husbands at home; for the husband is the head of the wife.

St. Paul

Men are superior to women on account of the qualities in which God has given them pre-eminence.

The Koran

In childhood a woman must be subject to her father; in youth to her husband; when her husband is dead, to her sons. A woman must never be free of subjugation.

The Hindu Code of Manu

Given the anti-woman prejudice in Christian, Moslem and Hindu scriptures, is it any wonder that in his morning prayer the Jewish male gives the following thanks:

Blessed art thou, oh Lord our God, King of the Universe, that I was not born a woman.

Woman-hating, which is granted the dignified term of misogyny, is an attitude that meets with wide social approval. It is so thoroughly acceptable an attitude that few women feel they are included in the insult when women as a group are ridiculed; in fact many will join in putting down other females, declaring that they dislike women and much prefer the company of men. The price to be paid for this acquiescence is that they too, being female, cannot escape the uneasy burden of self-hate.

On the other hand, although misogyny is an admired masculine stance, the idea of a woman who is a man-hater (there is no widely-used euphemism for this) sends chills down anyone's spine. It conjures up the image of a woman with spiked heels kicking a guy in the groin. It is one of the bitterest accusations hurled against the feminists.

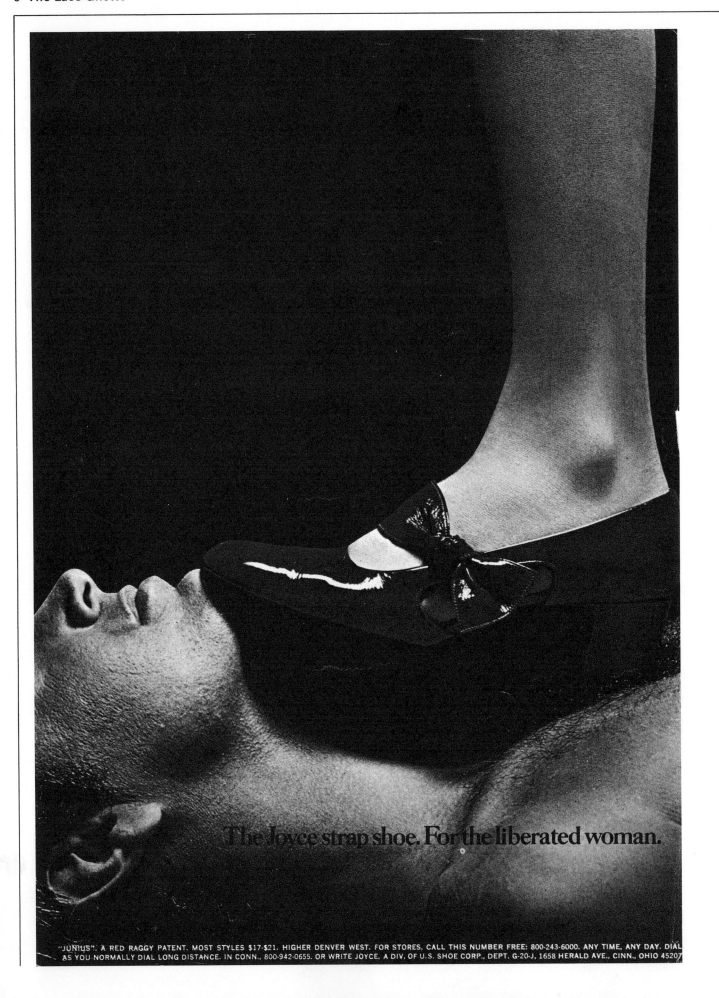

Society's view of woman, as expressed by those who have defined her, is not limited to glorifying her beauty or denying her full human status. Woman is also mother, she who brings forth new life. As we look for our own individual paths, we must come to terms with the ways in which we do differ biologically from men. A thorough understanding of our unique qualities need not limit our options, while it can help us to know ourselves. For that reason we are very fond of a quotation from one of the feminists' arch-villains, Norman Mailer.

Man is alienated from the nature which brought him forth. He is not, like woman, in possession of an inner space which gives her a link to the future.

Norman Mailer
The Prisoner of Sex

We in turn could define man by the phallic nature that is now linking him with outer space, the other side of the same mystery. Some truths, though, are reached by abandoning the intellect, and the Mailer quotation brings us to a deeper understanding of the essence of femaleness; but the issue is more complex—we are in possession of a human brain as well as a womb.

Woman can explore the universe intellectually, but man cannot carry a child within him. Perhaps—and this is just speculation—this fact underlies the resentment that causes some men, like Nietzsche, to see woman's link with nature through a horribly distorted vision.

What makes us respect and sometimes even fear a woman is her nature which is more "natural" than man's; her genuine jungle-like wily flexibility, her tiger's claw beneath the glove, her naive egoism, her uneducability and inward wildness, the incomprehensible wide sweep of her desires and virtues.

Friedrich Nietzsche

Nietzsche's statement is typical of the uncanny ability people have to project their own evil onto another who is somehow alien because not fully understood (i.e. Aryans to Jews, whites to blacks, men to women). Thus woman is often seen as a symbol of sin and temptation—the embodiment of a forbidden sexuality that, paradoxically, has been repressed in her for centuries.

There is a good principle which has created order, light and man; and a bad principle which has created chaos, darkness and woman.

Pythagoras

Woman is at once apple and serpent.

Heinrich Heine

This image of woman as evil is a powerful one— and some women prefer to be seen as a dark and mysterious, if evil, force rather than as subservient or victim. With all the power that has been projected onto woman in this way, men have had to make great efforts to keep her in an unthreatening position. The stereotype of woman as evil provides the justification for whatever means they employ.

One of the ways in which woman is rendered powerless is to be seen as a castrate, as a man with something missing in body and mind. In this view, woman with the tool of intellect is a ludicrous mutation— a fully human woman is a mistake.

Women of genius commonly have masculine faces, figures and manners. In transplanting brains to alien soil, God leaves a little of the original earth clinging to the roots.

Ambrose Bierce

I am very fond of the company of ladies. I like their beauty, I like their delicacy, I like their vivacity, and I like their silence.

Samuel Johnson

Women should be obscene and not heard.

John Lennon

A woman who is guided by the head and not by the heart is a social pestilence.

Honoré de Balzac

A woman with a masculine mind is not a being of superior efficiency; she is simply a phenomenon of imperfect differentiation—interestingly barren and without importance.

Joseph Conrad

What have they all been telling us?

Man is defined as a human being and woman is defined as female. Whenever she tries to behave as a human being she is accused of trying to emulate the male.

Simone de Beauvoir
The Second Sex

For centuries we have listened submissively to male voices telling us who we are. Recently the women's movement has begun to offer a female view of female existence; but we shouldn't assume that feminism began in the 1960's. As long ago as the eighteenth century, there were women who refused to accept restrictive definitions of themselves and fought for society's respect and a status of their own. The most determined of the feminist pioneers were the suffragettes of half a century ago.

The Queen is most anxious to enlist everyone to join in checking this mad, wicked folly of Women's Rights, with all its attendant horrors.... Woman would become the most hateful, heartless and disgusting of human beings were she allowed to unsex herself; and where would be the protection which man was intended to give the weaker sex? Queen Victoria

This mad wicked folly of Women's Rights or How we won the vote

"Give women the vote? But where will it all lead?" responded the Victorian male indignantly, his face slightly red, less from anger than from the confinement of his stiffly starched collar. "Next thing you know, they'll be wanting to wear pants."

Well, here we sit writing this book in jeans, the anti-suffragists' nightmare come true. What freedom we do have we owe largely to the women who fought for their sex's emancipation during the two previous centuries; their struggle for the vote was a product of a feminism that, from its beginnings, questioned the same assumptions about woman's role that are being challenged today.

THE NEW NURSE.

SENTINEL   CAPTAIN   COMMANDER IN CHIEF.

Women are told from their infancy and taught by the example of their mothers that a little knowledge of human weakness, justly termed cunning, softness of temper, outward obedience, and a scrupulous attention to a puerile kind of propriety, will obtain for them the protection of a man; and should they be beautiful everything else is needless for at least twenty years of their lives. . . .

Men, in their youth, are prepared for a profession, and marriage is not considered as the grand feature in their lives; whilst women, on the contrary, have no other scheme to sharpen their faculties or to rise in the world. They must marry advantageously, and to this object, their time is sacrificed and their person often legally prostituted.

> *Mary Wollstonecraft*
> Vindication of the Rights of Woman, 1795

In 1848, the Declaration of Sentiments passed at the Women's Rights Convention in Seneca Falls, New York, expressed resentment of the double sexual standard and commented on the damage done to woman's self-image.

The history of mankind is a history of repeated injuries and usurpations on the part of man toward woman, having in direct object the establishment of absolute tyranny over her. He has created false public sentiment by giving to the world a different code of morals for men than women, by which moral delinquincies which exclude women from society are not only tolerated but deemed of little account in men. He has endeavored in every way that he could to destroy her confidence in her powers, to lessen her self-respect, and to make her willing to lead a dependent and abject life.

If the position was bitter, it was understandably so. The statement was drafted by women who had just endured three days of a temperance conference, spending the entire time debating whether or not a woman member should be allowed to give a speech.

Today we have the vote (although many people, male and female, feel powerless even with it), but the basic issues of the women's rights struggle remain the same.

In this chapter we will deal less with the political mechanics of how the vote was won than with cultural attitudes to women in that era. The women's movement today cannot be seen as a completely new force, separate from what came before; it is a continuation of the same basic struggle waged by the suffragettes. Their major political demand was the vote, but, important as it was, it was a symbol of a more fundamental battle to liberate women on all levels.

Just over fifty years ago in Canada, women—along with idiots, lunatics, and criminals—were still denied the vote.

The nineteenth-century lady of the proper class and breeding saw that as part of the natural order. With her waist pinched in by steel or bone until it was no bigger than a man's arm, with hands not made for work and a brain not made for thinking, the ideal Victorian woman might have fit into more than one of the above categories.

Her survival depended upon her attracting a man through the fashion of the time. However, once she achieved her goal of a good marriage, she was, under British Common Law, legally dead. Early in the nineteenth century, the married woman had no right to own property, to sign contracts, or to make decisions concerning her children, who did not belong to her legally. She herself was entirely subject to her husband's rule, and wife-beating was permissible—if it was not done too severely.

Her mind was as imprisoned as her body. An educated woman was considered somehow "unnatural". When Elizabeth Blackwell, the first American woman to become a physician, was in medical school, the women who lived in her boarding house refused to speak to her and would pull their skirts aside so as not to touch her when they passed in the street. Woman was on a pedestal with a very narrow base.

A principal objection to women's rights was the argument that woman would be debased if she moved out of her ''sphere''. As Guillaume Amot, a Quebec M.P., said in 1894, woman is ''the point of connection between earth and Heaven. They assume something of the angel. . . . Let us leave them their moral purity, their bashfulness, their sweetness, which gave them in our minds so much charm.''

. . . Women who believe in woman suffrage seem to think that we men want to deprive them of their liberties; but we wish to do no such thing. All men who are worthy of the name of men, place woman upon a very high pedestal, to which no man, in his sphere, could ever hope to attain: and we want her to remain there, where she can command our respect and esteem and use the powers that God has given her for the good of humanity. . . . Why should she besmear herself with the rottenness of politics?

Letter to the Editor,
Toronto Globe, *1912*

Perhaps then, women of the working class were not really considered *human* females. They worked fourteen hours a day in mills and factories for lower wages than men. In mid-nineteenth-century England, women were used as coal pullers in mines, hitched to coal carts and dragging their load on all fours.

Betty Harris, Age 37: I have a belt around my waist and a chain passing between my legs, and I go on my hands and feet. The road is very steep, and we have to hold by a rope, and when there is no rope, by anything we can catch hold of. . . . It is very hard work for a woman. The pit is very wet where I work, and the water comes over our clogs always, and I have seen it up to my thighs: it rains in the roof terrible: my clothes are wet through almost all day long. . . . I am not so strong as I was, and cannot stand my work so well as I used to do. I have drawn till I have had the skin off me; the belt and chain is worse when we are in the family way.

from Wanda Neff,
Victorian Working Women

The police magistrate, in trying a fresh batch of prisoners, endeavours to arouse public indignation against the leaders of the movement by sternly rebuking them for allowing a mill girl of seventeen to come up from the provinces to assist in a London demonstration, in the course of which the girl was arrested. . . . She was a Lancashire delegate, representative of hundreds more who could not come themselves.

The magistrate was full of noble rage at "the cruelty of turning a girl of such tender age loose in London" as he expressed it. He seemed to count on setting men's hearts aflame at the base idea of a young girl in the streets without her mother. That she should be in the London streets to testify to her interests in the laws governing honest work, that was indeed shameful. "Why this child," he said, "should be in school."

The working women opened incredulous eyes. . . . They were stark amazed to find how strangely benighted are these great London gentlemen concerning the conditions governing the lives of women they make laws for. School at seventeen! Why this girl, like many more, had been earning her living in a mill since she was twelve, rising in the early dawn and tramping, cold and half-fed, to her work, and returning wearily through the slums whose haggard realism left the prematurely old "hand" of seventeen little to learn from London.

from Elizabeth Robbins,
"The Feminist Movement in England"
Colliers Magazine, ca. 1910

A SKETCH FROM NATURE.
Punch Publications, 1884

By the turn of the century England had about two million more women than men. Women who had previously been able to expect economic support from marriage were finding it necessary to seek work as governesses, typists and shopgirls.

According to Canadian suffragist Nellie McClung, 30 per cent of the women in North America at the time were working—most out of financial need. In 1912 there were 46,000 women employed in Toronto alone, out of a female population of about 190,000. Women believed that if they got the vote they could demand and get equal pay for equal work with men. Trade unionists often supported women's demands for the vote because their low wages were undercutting men on the labour market.

It seems hard to believe that woman herself has clung to her chains of slavery, and instead of encouraging and assisting the brave torchbearers who have prepared the way for a broader and nobler womanhood to be possible, she has often drawn her skirts around her and whimpered, "I am perfectly satisfied to be the power behind the throne. A woman's place is in her home," etc., forgetting that many women would have no homes if they had not got out and hustled to keep themselves and their children.

Flora MacDonald Denison
Toronto Suffrage Association, ca. 1909

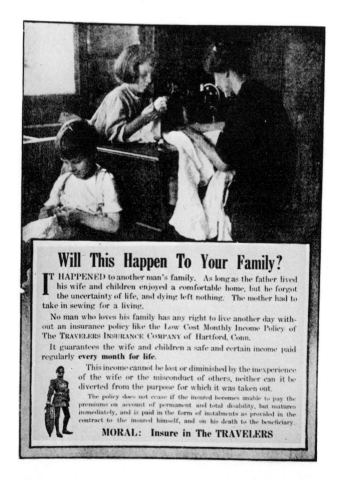

Will This Happen To Your Family?

IT HAPPENED to another man's family. As long as the father lived his wife and children enjoyed a comfortable home, but he forgot the uncertainty of life, and dying left nothing. The mother had to take in sewing for a living.

No man who loves his family has any right to live another day without an insurance policy like the Low Cost Monthly Income Policy of The TRAVELERS INSURANCE COMPANY of Hartford, Conn.

It guarantees the wife and children a safe and certain income paid regularly **every month for life.**

This income cannot be lost or diminished by the inexperience of the wife or the misconduct of others, neither can it be diverted from the purpose for which it was taken out.

The policy does not cease if the insured becomes unable to pay the premiums on account of permanent and total disability, but matures immediately, and is paid in the form of instalments as provided in the contract to the insured himself, and on his death to the beneficiary.

MORAL: Insure in The TRAVELERS

Politicians frequently used the argument that women themselves did not want the vote. Even Canadian suffragist Helena Gutteridge admitted in 1915, "The backwardness of the suffragette movement . . . is not due . . . to the desire of men to dominate their women-folk, but to the lack of interest displayed by the women themselves."

Of course, we are still being told that women are lacking in logic, are more emotional and weaker in demanding situations than men. In fact, it is these very qualities that still define "feminine", something a strong, logical woman supposedly is not. Women are encouraged to develop these traits from the time they are children; it is a part of the process of sex-role socialization with which we will deal in Chapter 3.

Hysteria and obscure "women's ailments" were characteristic of Victorian women who had to take to bed instead of the psychiatrist's couch. Cures for these female diseases were a thriving business. Lydia Pinkham's Vegetable Compound was 18 per cent alcohol, and probably did ease many discomforts.

We now know that hysteria is often a product of repression—sexual or otherwise. A swig of 18-per-cent-alcohol medicine could quickly make a women forget the normal drives of sex, of power, of the intellect, that were taboo in her society.

But even if women were sometimes their own worst enemies, men often were strong allies.

It will be generally conceded that man consults or obeys woman, not only because she is his mate, but because he finds her his spiritual complement—sometimes his spiritual superior. He sees her tender and self-sacrificing, earnest and pure, beautiful in form and in soul and sets her on a shrine above the sordid rough-and-tumble world of competition and avarice in which, perforce, he must spend laborious days. Further, he thinks her a prophetess, divinely illuminated, able to discern wisdom and truth by some mysterious gift of intuition more awful and compelling than his own slow methods of syllogism or induction. Lastly . . . woman in the eyes of man is always the mother: mother of his children, still perhaps unborn, the mother who in his early, impressionable years of early childhood set his feet in the path of good and evil, which he still treads today. Woman as mother, sweetheart, inspirer and friend, man accepts and welcomes.

But once she despises these relations, once she ceases to be what he thinks and wishes, once she begins to invade his province, to think his thoughts and to do his work, then there will be a great revolt from female ascendancy, actual or threatened. Then men will point out that women cannot reason, and that politics for instance must be guided by reason; that woman is emotion and that government by emotion quickly degenerates into injustice; that woman, however excellent as a student, is lacking in genius, in initiative, in the power of forming abstract opinions. . . . On all these points, I fear, man has only to appeal to science and history to prove his case.

> *Clementine Fessenden*
> *Letter to the Editor,*
> Toronto Mail and Empire, *1912*

While it is true that women were unfairly dealt with in matters of education, until recently, that day is past, and now the world over, well-educated women are doing good work. . . . Woman has her place and man has his, and many vocations long considered as belonging to men are now rightfully entered upon by women such as clerical work of many kinds. . . .

[However,] physically, I contend, they are unfit for the strain of political life. Neither do I consider that woman has the power of mental grasp necessary for the consideration of large questions of business, world-wide commerce, diplomatic relations of nations, controlling of armaments by sea and land, and others, and yet, if she takes the reigns these must be dealt with.

Since the world began, statesmanship has been man's prerogative. Woman by all the laws of nature has a right to be his helpmate. . . .

> *Marian Boultbee*
> *Letter to the Editor,*
> Toronto Globe, *1912*

I fear some of the women who scream for votes are the women whose opinion is not valued by men . . . I maintain that women without the vote are a powerful factor, but women are too impulsive to be given the legislation, and may I add, too hysterical. The woman who rises above the weaknesses of her sex is fit for the vote . . . but we must not forget the women who are bundles of nerves and yet if once we had the vote, they would have it equally. But I fear also I am a woman and only scratch the surface.

> *"A Descendant of Eve"*
> *Letter to the Editor,*
> Toronto Globe, *1912*

I no longer ask myself whether woman is fit to vote. I begin to consider whether she is fit to live. Obviously on her merits (if she can be said to have any merits) she is not. . . . Man is, as everybody knows, always efficient, reasonable, well balanced. . . . Woman is not really wanted except for one oversight, which made the services of this deplorable sex requisite for the perpetuation of the race. Science will no doubt, in due course, remedy this defect and enable the necessary function to be performed by other agencies. Why on earth should we be pestered with a million persons, perennial invalids, potential lunatics, possible suffragists?

. . . A certain number of women seem still required to discharge various humble and mostly unpleasant tasks, at a low rate of payment. Somebody must wash clothes, sew on shirt buttons, scrub and sweep the dust. You cannot abase the dignity of the male by setting him to these tasks, and if you did you would have to pay him too much. I suppose too, some women must be allowed to act as nurses in hospital wards, and to look after the sponges and dressings when great surgeons perform operations for enviable fees. For these reasons we cannot hope for a deliverance from an "epicene" world all at once.

> *Letter to a London newspaper by Sidney Low,*
> *quoted in the Letters to the Editor of the*
> Toronto Mail & Empire, *September 13, 1912,*
> *by Adeline C. Roberts*

Over and over again, even today, women are told that they should be content to use their "influence" for good, without attempting a more direct method of bringing about reforms. . . . Gentleness and tact are both admirable qualities for a woman to possess, but pushed to an extreme they degenerate into weakness and readiness to obtain desirable ends by doubtful means; and it is hardly fair to women that they should so often find the direct, straightforward road deliberately blocked against them, and that they should be forced in consequence—often to the detriment of their strength of character—to work by circuitous and indirect methods.

Editorial,
Toronto Globe, *November 6, 1912*

Woman Less Truthful than Man. More than One~Half of the Lies That Women Tell Are Due to Her Gentleness

Does woman really lie more than man? Yes, unquestionably, yes . . . undoubtedly due to her gentleness, her consideration, her sympathy—in short, to the goodness of her heart.

Woman lies in many little things simply because she is woman. She lies with the whole of her person. She transforms herself with the changes of fashion, as if she were a piece of soft metal that is put over and over again into the melting pot and recast. . . .

I know a very pretty and fascinating lady, one of the best wives and mothers that I have ever encountered on my road through life. Her husband, after twenty-odd years of wedlock is as much in love with her as when they were married and she with him. She once confided to me the price that she had paid for his still youthful passion.

"He has never seen me cross, or even depressed. He has never seen me with my hair out of order or carelessly dressed. Even when I have the most fearful headache I pretend that nothing is wrong. No matter how ill and tired I may be, or what worries I have, if he wishes me to go with him to the theatre or to a party, I dress at once, and do everything I can to look radiant."

This wife, perhaps, has never told her husband a falsehood but is not her conduct a continual lie?

Maclean's Magazine, *June 1913*

YOU MUSTN'T ASK TO VOTE

You may be our close companion
    Share our troubles, ease our pain,
You may bear the servant's burden
    (But without the servant's gain;)
You may scrub and cook and iron
    Sew the buttons on our coat,
But as men we must protect you—
    You are far too frail to vote.

You may toil behind our counters,
    In our factories you may slave
You are welcome in the sweatshop
    From the cradle to the grave.
If you err, altho' a woman
    You may dangle by the throat
But our chivalry is outraged
    If you soil your hands to vote.

L. Case Russell
from the Toronto Globe, *September 28, 1912*

Woman was told that she did not need political power because she commanded the art of loving persuasion. Her subtle wiles were more effective than the ballot. This "pussycat" tactic still meets with great favour today, since it is considered more "feminine" than directness. But even in the era of the suffragettes some were aware of its detrimental effect on women.

One of the most powerful weapons used against the suffragettes was ridicule. Women who asked for the vote were portrayed as mannish, frustrated, hysterical cranks.

When a newspaper wishes to disprove a woman's contention or demolish her theories, it draws ugly pictures of her. If it can show that she has big feet or red hands or wears unbecoming clothes, that certainly settles the case and puts her where she belongs.

Nellie McClung
In Times Like These

Or they were seen as truly feminine little lambs
being adorably inept at playing suffragette.

TEN LITTLE SUFFRAGETTES

TEN little SUFFRAGETTES, arranged in battle line
  One saw a bargain sale and then there were but nine.
NINE little SUFFRAGETTES, in a fighting state
  One lost her servant girl and then there were but eight.
EIGHT little SUFFRAGETTES, by angry fervor driven
  One went to the manicure's, and then there were but seven.
SEVEN little SUFFRAGETTES, armed with stones and bricks
  One had matinee seats, and then there were but six.
SIX little SUFFRAGETTES, determined still to strive
  One's new gown did not come home, and then there were but five.
FIVE little SUFFRAGETTES, parading as to war
  One's shoes began to pinch and then there were but four.
FOUR little SUFFRAGETTES still craving to be free
  One found a milliner's, and then there were but three.
THREE little SUFFRAGETTES, resolved to see it through
  One got an auto car, and then there were but two.
TWO little SUFFRAGETTES, their mission yet undone,
  One couldn't hook her waist, and then there was but one.
ONE little SUFFRAGETTE, still answering to the call
  She got married, and there were none at all.

Paul West
New York World

    A letter to the Editor of the Toronto *Mail & Empire*,
December 13, 1911, written after a visit to Toronto
by Emmeline Pankhurst, illustrates the patronizing attitude of the time: "If all women were as likely to
make intelligent use of the ballot as Mrs. Pankhurst
there would be no hesitation about granting the demand
to the suffragettes, and probably each reader knows
at least one child who would make a wiser voter than
the average man. Nevertheless, we do not hear any
particular demand for the enfranchisement of children."
    But women were as serious about getting the vote
as any other oppressed group. Violence had always
been a political tool for men. In England the Women's
Social and Political Union (W.S.P.U.), led by Emmeline
Pankhurst and her daughters Christabel and Sylvia,
ignored or double-crossed by the politicians, met
the frustration of their aims first with civil disobedience,
and, when that failed, with militant action.

EXPLOSIVES FOUND IN MILITANTS' FLAT

Interesting Exhibits Before a London Magistrate

REFUSES OFFERS OF BAIL

Two of the Suffragettes Became So Noisy During the Hearing That They Had to be Removed—Eight Released From Holloway Jail.

London, May 26 [1914] The suffragette prisoners arrested by the police during a raid on a west-end flat on May 21 were brought before the magistrate today.

Nellie Hall and Grace Roe became so uproarious in the prisoners' enclosure that they had to be removed and during the process kicked and shrieked at the top of their voices. Nellie Hall shouted:

"I have been forcibly fed twice daily and am nearly dead as a result."

She seemed half demented as she struggled with the police. Her hat was torn off, her clothes disarranged and her hair dishevelled.

"You devils, you beasts!" she shrieked and was carried out of the court to the cells.

The Toronto Globe, *May 27, 1914*

Nellie Hall in 1914, age 20

Mrs. Nell Hall-Humpherson, today at 78

Robin Knight

Nellie Hall, now Mrs. Nell Hall-Humpherson, lives in Toronto. She was a militant organizer for the W.S.P.U. which she joined at the age of sixteen. Her mother was one of the original six members of the group and her father, Leonard Hall, was the first vice-president of the British Labour Party. She is still an active member of the Association of Women Electors in Toronto.

Mrs. Hall-Humpherson: *When I was at one school the headmistress, who had been top of everything at Oxford, said to me: "You know, I find it very irritating because my gardener can't write his own name, can't read, and he has the vote and I haven't." Some time later, when I was sixteen, I was arrested for the first time. When I got back to school the next day after the trial, she wasn't at all pleased. We were walking up and down the assembly hall and she was telling me that the end didn't justify the means—and then down the staircase came a flying figure in a gown. It was the headmaster. He came and put his hands out and said: "My dear, how proud I am of you!"*

What were you doing the first time you were arrested?
It was about the time of the first forcible feedings. And I wasn't really doing anything. There was a meeting about Lloyd George's Insurance Bill, and they had cordoned off the street leading to the place almost two weeks before. But the women were already in the street. You see, they had posed as charwomen and went out every morning so that the police would get used to them. Well, they got into the building and it was just pandemonium. I don't know how many women were arrested.

How did you get involved in the more militant aspects of the struggle?
One day my mother was supposed to go and break some windows. Prime Minister Asquith was coming to make a speech to the Jewellers' Association of Birmingham. But she was taken very ill and was saying: "Oh, what am I going to do." I said: "Oh, I'll go for you," and she answered: "Your father will have a fit." But off I went.
*   You could hear smashing glass all over the place and the man next to me said: "You know what I'd love to do—I'd love to get hold of one of those women. I know what I'd do with 'em." Well, I got one of the bricks and threw it through a plate glass window belonging to some stockbrokers—the biggest plate glass window in the neighbourhood.*

It was rather an upper-class woman that was involved in the suffragette movement, wasn't it?

H. M. Prison Holloway

May 23ʳᵈ 1904.

Dear ~~████████~~ Father!

I am now in this Prison, and am in _____ health.

I am remanded without bail until

If I behave well, I shall be allowed to write another letter about

Tuesday. I send my deepest love.

_____ and to receive a reply, but no reply is

allowed to this.

Signature— Nell.

Register No. 18686

Not always, no. There were many wealthy women but also some very poor ones. We were really a very mixed lot.

Because it's been said that it was an intellectual and bourgeois movement, never really a popular movement. *Oh it was. I know in Birmingham, more than two-thirds, at least, of the members were women who earned their own living, who were all working at jobs that men did and weren't getting the same money.*

When did the militancy start?
It started after a political meeting in 1905 when Sir Edward Grey, Secretary of State for Foreign Affairs, wouldn't answer our questions. You'd write the question out, send the question up, and they wouldn't take any notice of it. Then you'd get up and ask the question and you'd be thrown out. Well, this got rather tiresome, being thrown out all the time. I think it was about then that we decided to set fire to the pillar [mail] boxes.

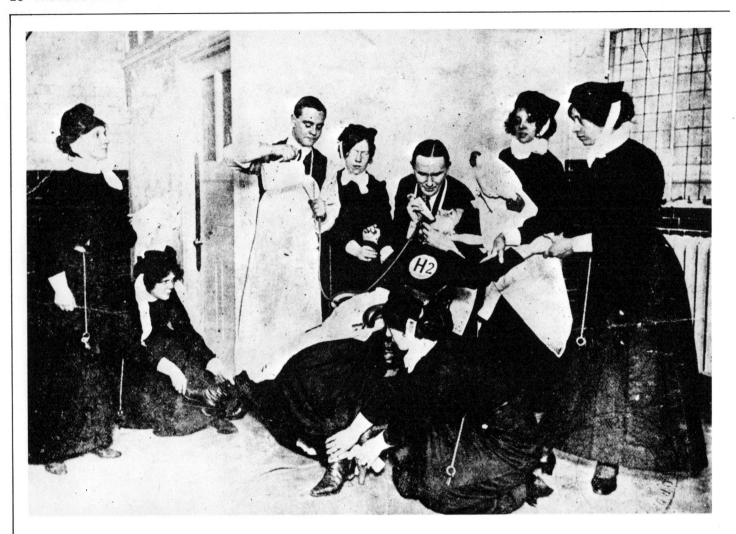

Is it true that Mrs. Pankhurst ordered you all that not a cat or a canary should be harmed in the bombings? *We were told that nothing but our own lives was to be endangered—the trouble I went to trying to find an empty house without a caretaker, the telegrams I sent saying that somebody was ill, to get them out of the house. . . .*

What about the stories of horsewhipping of men, for instance Winston Churchill? Are they true? *Oh yes, quite true. Once I had to arrange it at a wedding. It was Asquith who was to be horsewhipped, but they got the wrong man. It turned out to be the Senior Commissioner of Scotland Yard. But I didn't mind that. It served him right, too.*

Women were weak and had to be protected. That was why they shouldn't have the vote. But they certainly weren't too weak to be thrown into British prisons. Inside prison, the suffragettes continued their struggle by going on hunger strikes. The authorities retaliated with the brutal process of forcible feeding.

Dearest Mother,
I am fighting, fighting, fighting. I have four, five or six wardresses every day as well as two doctors. I am fed through the stomach tube twice a day. They pry open my mouth with a steel gag, pressing it in where there is a gap in my teeth. I resist all the time. My gums are always bleeding. I am afraid they may be saying that we do not resist, yet my shoulders are bruised by the struggling while they hold the tube in my throat. I used to feel that I should go mad at first and be pretty near to it, as I think they feared, but I have got over that, and my digestion is the thing most likely to suffer now.

"Sylvia" [Pankhurst]

Nellie Hall was one of the hunger strikers who was forcibly fed.

Mrs. Hall-Humpherson: *It's a . . . a terrible experience.*
I think probably the worst part of it was the assault.
I didn't know how painful it would be. I'd heard about
the tube but I didn't know what happened. I had as many
as twelve wardresses. The cell could hardly hold them
all. They would hold my legs and feet. The nurse would
put her fingers—her little fingers—in the corner of
your eyes so that you couldn't move your head without
getting your eyes poked in.

I had the tube down my throat but other women had
it put down their noses. I think that must have been
excruciating . . . just terrible. I couldn't bear that.

Were many women injured by forcible feeding?
Oh, yes. The last time I was at Mrs. Pankhurst's birth-
day celebration there was a woman there who's still
lame from it.

One of the most tragic occurrences during that period
was the death of Emily Wilding Davidson who threw
herself under the King's horse at the Derby and was
killed. Did she intend to kill herself?
Oh, no. She must have known, though, that she might
be killed. Just as the horses came around she grabbed
the first horse that she could reach. It happened to be
the King's horse. Some of the other horses panicked . . .
they took her off the track to give her first aid. Then
they took her away to a hospital and she died there.
She never recovered consciousness.

As a matter of fact I was going to meet her that after-
noon because I had something that she wanted. I still
have it because I never saw her again. It was an address
book. A beautiful one of hand-tooled leather. She had
seen it in a bazaar and admired it and I said to myself
that I'd get it for her. I still have it.

Did the onlookers know who she was and why she did
that?
Yes. She had the colours on. She was wearing the sash
—purple, green and white.

How were you all regarded by most of the people? As
freaks of some sort?
Oh, by most, yes.

Unladylike creatures?
Oh, unladylike, yes, most certainly.

Do you think there's a need for militancy on the part
of women today?
Well, I thought the women who went to Ottawa to
protest about abortion and made a scene in the chamber
were wrong. That's an act of breaking the law and I
think they should be treated as people who break the
law.

Yet you were breaking the law when you were smashing windows.
No, no, no, no.

Weren't you?
No. Because we had no part in making the law. You see, this was a very strong position to have. None of us felt we were breaking the law. I think it's very damaging and can have terrible repercussions. Even if change takes a long time it's worthwhile to do it peacefully. And more change has taken place in the last fifty years than in perhaps the past thousand.

WHAT WOMEN WANT TO SET RIGHT

Women are expected to pay taxes and obey the laws, yet have no voice in saying what those laws and taxes shall be.

In the eyes of the law the married woman is not the parent of her own child. In cases of separation the children are given into the custody of the father, unless it can be proved that he is not a fit person to have them.

Women only own their illegitimate children, and are alone responsible for their education and maintenance.

Women in industrial or professional life of any nature are not given equal pay for equal work with men.

Women do not own one cent of their dower rights until after their husbands are dead.

The age of consent for women in Ontario at 16 is too low. In one Canadian Province it is 14.

The Child Labor law age limit of 12 years is too young.

When women want to do anything in the State they cannot achieve their ends directly—they must have some one do it for them.

The failure of men legislators to stamp out the white slave traffic.

Toronto Star Weekly, March 23, 1913

There were no fire bombs thrown in the name of woman's suffrage in Canada, where the movement got off to an embarrassingly timid start. The first suffrage organization, founded in 1876, called itself the Toronto Women's Literary Club. By 1883, however, they had grown bolder and renamed themselves the Toronto Women's Suffrage Association.

But the founder of the movement, Dr. Emily Howard Stowe, was a more courageous woman than that brief history would indicate. Emily Howard Stowe was Canada's first female doctor. Faced with the problem of supporting her family when her husband became ill, she decided to become a physician. But no Canadian medical school would accept a woman at that time and she had to receive her training in the United States.

In the two decades after the "Literary Club" was formed, suffrage groups sprang up all over the country; there was also a national organization, with headquarters in Toronto, whose most prominent members were Dr. Augusta Stowe-Gullen, daughter of Dr. Emily Howard Stowe, Sonia Leathes, and Flora MacDonald Denison.

The Canadian women preferred to be called "suffragists" as opposed to "suffragettes", which referred to the women who threw bricks and knew their way around explosives. However, the Canadian women for the most part did support their militant sisters in England.

After Flora MacDonald Denison visited the W.S.P.U. in London, she commented to the press: "There is a great drama being enacted in London at the present time. In the play, there is a villain and a clown, both of which characters are played by one man, the British government. The hero is Mrs. Pankhurst."

Mrs. Denison was also of the opinion that Mrs. Pankhurst's tactics were quite successful and remarked that before the militancy was adopted, no notice whatever had been taken of the women's suffrage unions or their carefully worded petitions. She felt the militancy in England had a great effect in helping the suffrage cause in Canada and the U.S.

The Canadian suffrage movement was composed primarily of professional women, business women, and the wives of the well-to-do. One of their reasons for wanting the vote was to eliminate some of the ugly social problems they saw around them. They were not, like some British suffragettes such as Sylvia Pankhurst, socialists who saw the roots of social inequity in the political and economic structure of the country. But the Canadian women did see the need for reform of the most visibly appalling conditions. Thus granting women the vote in Canada was a factor in bringing about new child-labour laws and better factory conditions.

At this point we must admit that the Women's Christian Temperance Union was an important part of the Canadian suffrage movement, except in Quebec. The prohibition issue was often cited by "dries" (or "wets") as a reason to give (or not give) women the vote. The W.C.T.U. is often seen as an embodiment of the ethic "if it feels good it must be bad for you," but in fact they were naive, well-meaning reformers attempting to rid the country of the evils of demon rum, which they felt wrecked many working-class homes and kept the men from "bettering" themselves. Unfortunately, they did not ask what made these men turn to drink in the first place.

Anti-suffrage groups were also formed. In the U.S. these groups were largely run and financed by brewers and distillers who feared that female suffrage would mean more votes for the "dries". It has been claimed that the prohibition movement delayed woman suffrage by two generations in the United States. This was true, at least in part, in Canada as well.

One stain on the record of the American and Canadian suffrage movements was an attitude that we now recognize as biased along race and class lines. At a time when "Negroes" and "Orientals" and "foreigners" who were ill-educated and of the lower classes could vote, here were "cultured", white, middle-class women who could not. James L. Hughes, a prominent member of the Dominion Women's Enfranchisement Association, wrote: "Sex slavery is more indefensible than race or class slavery, and the complete emancipation of woman will be a grander triumph for justice and truth and liberty than the granting of freedom to any race or class in the history of the world."

We want to protect our homes. The chief danger is not from an enemy without but from the enemies of drink, ignorance, disease and crime within. These are what cause the fall of nations. . . .

In this township we tried to protect our homes from the evils of the drink traffic this year but failed to get the three-fifths majority. It was due chiefly to the votes of worthless heads of homes and worthless hangers-on in hotels with no stake in the country. This would not have happened if mothers had the vote as well as fathers.

We want our men to strengthen the native Canadian vote, because of the flood of immigration that is coming in. Ignorant, unfit weaklings from Europe and China are enfranchised, and at the present rate of immigration will swamp the vote of Canadian men. The well-educated, hard working, thoughtful women of Ontario will have to be ruled by these. . . .

"One of your country readers"
Letter to the Editor
Toronto Globe, *1912*

In Canada, as in the U.S., the vote was won first in the west. In the prairies, the women's movement had the widespread support of men, including most farmers' organizations. No one could tell a pioneer woman she was too delicate to vote. In 1916, Manitoba became the first province in Canada to give women the vote. It was achieved primarily through the dull, tedious, hard work of securing signatures on petitions, the condition upon which the Liberals promised to make female suffrage a party plank. The Liberals won the election and the women won the vote, ousting Premier Sir Rodmond Roblin who had once said: "I don't want a hyena in petticoats talking politics to me. I want a nice gentle creature to bring me my slippers."

WHEN THE VOTE WAS WON

Manitoba	January 28, 1916
Saskatchewan	March 14, 1916
Alberta	April 19, 1916
British Columbia	April 5, 1917
Ontario	April 12, 1917
Nova Scotia	April 26, 1918
New Brunswick	April 17, 1919
Prince Edward Island	May 3, 1922
Newfoundland	April 13, 1925
Quebec	April 25, 1940

On the federal level women were enfranchised in three steps, the first two being ploys to keep Sir Robert Borden's Conservative government in power. The first was the Military Voters Act of 1917, which gave the vote to all British subjects, male or female, who had been active in any branch of the Canadian Armed Forces; this included a number of women who were nurses. The second was the Wartime Elections Act of 1917, a piece of legislation that was widely abhorred. It served to disenfranchise large portions of the population which might not have been inclined to re-elect the Borden government. These were conscientious objectors (including Doukhobors and Mennonites), those of enemy alien birth and all citizens of European birth speaking an enemy alien language who had become naturalized Canadian citizens after 1902. The act did give the franchise to all female British subjects over the age of twenty-one who had a husband, brother or father serving in the Canadian Armed Forces—thus winning more votes in the 1917 general election for the government's war policies, especially conscription.

For reasons of political expediency the government had partially enfranchised women. It could no longer justify not giving all women the vote when the war ended. In 1918 the government drew up a bill granting the vote to all Canadian women over the age of twenty-one. As originally drafted, women would have achieved wider suffrage than men in Quebec, where there was still a property qualification for voting. The bill was therefore amended to read that women would qualify under the same stipulations as men in each province.

On October 18, 1929, Canadian women became *people* by a decision of the Supreme Court of Canada. This reversed an earlier decision that women were not "persons" within the meaning of the British North America Act. Said Nellie McClung, "The news came as a complete shock to many women who had not known they were not persons until they heard it stated that they were."

The struggle for this basic recognition had begun in 1916 when Emily Ferguson Murphy, Canada's first woman magistrate, named to family court in Edmonton, was told by the lawyer of a man she had sentenced on her first day in court that the decision was not valid, because she was not a "person" and therefore had no legal status as a magistrate.

QUEBEC LADIES HAIL VICTORY OF ONTARIO WOMEN

Think it Will Not Be Long Now Before They are Given the Vote in This Province — War Has Opened Eyes of Many

The province of Quebec stands out as a barrier in the way of Canada's movement towards universal suffrage. For the women of Quebec, the question did not end with the federal franchise of 1918; it was not until 1940, twenty-two years later, that they were given the vote by the province. And for a long period after that they were tightly restricted by the province's ancient Civil Code. Not until 1965 could Quebec married women own property, control their own bank accounts, or share in the guardianship of children, which meant that a mother had not power of consent in matters such as children's marriages or hospital operations.

. . . Other provinces marching rapidly in the wake of the Federal government have given women the vote. Quebec has not yet fallen into that supremely unfortunate error. . . . The origin of the woman's movement . . . springs from . . . the negation of man's authority. It is the negation of the authority of the home which demands that every household shall submit to the authority of the father.

> Action Catholique *(organ of the church party and Cardinal Bevan)*

Premier Taschereau . . . said that the Latin mentality . . . did not look kindly on women voting . . . and the Latin mentality prevails in Quebec.

> Montreal Free Press
> *February 16, 1922*

I don't believe granting women the vote would benefit the province at all, and furthermore, I am of the opinion that the great majority of the women of Quebec do not want the vote.

> *Premier Taschereau, March 10, 1928*

Le progrès des nations se mesure par le développement de l'esprit de justice, la conquête de l'égoisme, le respect de la liberté et des droits des individus.

Idola St. Jean, leader of L'Alliance canadienne pour le vote des femmes de Québec

Mme. Thérèse Casgrain was one of the leaders of Quebec's women's-rights struggle. In 1951 she became the first woman to lead a political party when she was elected president of the Quebec Social Democratic Party. She was appointed a Senator in 1970.

Mme. Casgrain: *In Quebec we could vote federally, we could choose the prime minister of Canada, but we had nothing to say with regard to the prime minister of Quebec. You could be a senator since '29, you could be elected to the House of Commons, but in the province of Quebec you were absolutely a minor. You couldn't do anything, especially if you were married. There was a charming article in our Civil Code until 1965, Article 188, where they said the husband could take a separation against his wife if she were guilty of adultery but* she *couldn't unless he kept his concubine in the house. They said that of course the moral offense was the same for men and women but it was more painful for the heart of the man.*

Why did it take women so long to get the vote in Quebec?
You know, it's one of the queerest things. I'm trying to explain it to myself because in the early part of the nineteenth century the women of Quebec were considered persons and were allowed to vote. It was the only part of the British empire where this strange custom was accepted. I remember the mother of Joseph Papineau who voted for her son because she said he was a good and honest citizen. Well, by 1834 women were not using their vote because of public opinion and in 1849 it was legally taken away from them.

In 1927 there was a split in the Quebec women's movement. Mlle. Idola St. Jean broke away from the Provincial Franchise Committee and formed *L'Alliance canadienne pour le vote des femmes de Québec.* It had deeper roots among working-class people and was more strictly a French organization. Said Mlle. St. Jean about the Committee: "The only activity of the said Committee during five years of existence consisted in a few meetings and a reception given to Lady Astor."
In 1940 Mme. Casgrain, then president of the Provincial Franchise Committee, and Mlle. St. Jean were described in the Montreal *Standard* of March 23: "These remarkable women have long been the spearhead of woman suffrage in Quebec. They are not of a sameness. Flexible, witty and charming to her fingertips, Mme. Casgrain has been the suffrage rapier; grim, relentless, implacable as the rock of Adamant, Mlle. St. Jean has been the suffrage saber."

What did that description of you both mean?
Well, it meant division and that was a little unfortunate, because Mlle. St. Jean had some wonderful qualities, and, of course, it always affects any movement if you haven't got unity. But she would come with us and we would join forces in public action, so that was good. She did a good job. And she would be there each time we'd ask for suffrage.

Unfortunately, the members of the House would pick on her and make nasty remarks. Poor Miss St. Jean was unmarried and had no children and she was at times perhaps a bit bitter. One of the members was so rude once it was simply terrible. He said, "If Miss St. Jean is not pleased I can give her my pants." You see, they did not take it seriously. They joked about it and they made nasty comments. They began to take it seriously though, when they became afraid it was coming through.

What caused the fear?
Their prejudices were so strong. Oddly enough, a lot of English people were delighted because they thought, well, we lost it in England and in the U.S. Let's keep woman in her place in Quebec.

Do you think there's still a fight to be waged?
I'm never satisfied. We have only one woman in the House of Commons. We have very few women professors. Have you seen many women editors? Have you any women at the top in CBC? Even in M. Lévesque's Parti Québecois, which is supposed to be so radical—there are five men on the executive and not one single woman.

Why is that? Is it prejudice? Or is it the women themselves?
I think a lot of women are afraid.

Can this be improved by the individual or do you need organizations?
Well, I think that you have to organize not as women but as human beings, because men can help us a lot. Curiously enough, the men who have no inferiority complex, who are not afraid of our competition, never have any objections. There were many fine men who helped us win suffrage.

Was it prejudice that kept women from having the vote for so long in Quebec?
Yes, prejudice. And passivity on the part of women. Because they were resigned—and they still are resigned. Not only in Quebec, mind you. In Canada they are pretty bad, too.

We have been ill-prepared for the rights that were fought for so hard. In the following chapter on female socialization we will see how women are taught to be dependent, encouraged to remain childlike, protected from the very challenges that would allow us to become mature and independent beings—persons who can meet life head-on and not shrink from it.

Socialization

A little boy, maybe seven years old, runs out of the house, hockey stick in hand, and down the street to where the usual group of kids are standing around. Some of them hail him with shouts as they see him approaching. They're waiting to start the daily ritual game of street hockey. Quickly, almost automatically, they take their regular positions on the road, ready to play. But just before the game begins, the boy looks up and sees that some of the kids aren't playing. As a matter of fact, he suddenly thinks, they never play. For just a moment he wonders why. But then, with a blink of recognition he remembers—they're the girls.

From the earliest ages girls and boys are aware that they are different from each other behaviourally as well as physically. To a boy, a girl is someone you can't horse around with because she always ends up crying; she also gets in trouble if she dirties her clothes. To a girl, a boy is someone who is reckless, messy and disobedient. Of course there are exceptions. But generally, most young children are vitally aware of these standard differences in personality.

How do the differences in masculine-feminine characteristics come about? Do men emerge from the womb with genetic patterns bearing such assorted qualities as courage, logic, talent, and the divine right of authority? Are women biologically preordained to unfold as sweet, sensitive, yielding, and only whimsically intelligent? Not exactly. From the time female babies are wrapped in pink and male babies in blue, the personality differences between them are basically learned.

One is not born, but rather becomes, a woman. No biological, psychological or economic fate determines the figure that the human female presents in society; it is civilization as a whole that produces this creature, intermediate between male and eunuch, which is described as feminine.

Simone de Beauvoir
The Second Sex

As infants we begin life with no innate ideas of the social order that surrounds us; we look for clues to guide us in perceiving both ourselves and our environment. We do not witness the world directly, but through a filter of images, ideas and conventions that we have learned. This is a major part of a very necessary process known as socialization; without it we would have no reference points—no criteria with which to choose among the infinite possibilities that exist. Socialization eases our relations within society.

And through this almost unconscious guidance we learn what it means to be a woman or a man. But it is becoming more and more evident that the feminine and masculine roles, as they are assigned at present, are extremely restrictive, limiting the personal development of women, as well as men.

Whatever the "real" differences between the sexes may be, we are not likely to know them until the sexes are treated differently, that is alike. And this is very far from being the case at present.

Kate Millett
Sexual Politics

So, you may ask, is there really anything wrong with encouraging girls to act "just like a girl" and boys to act "just like a boy"? What's wrong with teaching them very separate modes of behaviour?

Fem-i-nine (adj.) like a woman; weak; gentle.

**The Random House Dictionary
of the English Language**

In such a manner are we defined, and through socialization we internalize this definition in ourselves, we become what is expected of us. Weak is indisputably a very unflattering adjective—yet we learn to accept that that is what we are—by definition, inferior.

Children are aided in interpreting their environment by parents, teachers, television, books that are bought for them, and by other children with whom they are in contact. This direction of a child's vision is constant, yet it is so pervasive and so widely accepted that until recently we have been unaware of its real nature.

Boys fix things.

Girls need things fixed.

From I'm Glad I'm a Boy! I'm Glad I'm a Girl!
© 1970 by Windmill Books © 1970 by Whitney Darrow, Jr.

Is such blatant role-playing still taken for granted and almost unthinkingly passed on to children? To try and discover the extent of male-female socialization, we interviewed students at a *progressive* elementary school in a Toronto suburb. Some of their statements, which appear throughout this chapter, read like a feminist's nightmare—indicating the astonishing degree to which children's minds have been (and are continuing to be) set into strict masculine and feminine patterns even at the early ages. Nine children, ranging in age from four to nine, were selected at random. Their words are their own.*

* Helping to interview these children was a group of ten older students at the same school involved in a study of women's and children's liberation. They were: Danny Bakan, John Bakan, Debbie Garland, Mark Halpern, Sandra Levin, Cindy Rotenberg, Ricki Schojnacki, Michael Sylvester and Jamie Waese.

Have you ever thought of being a doctor?

Carol, 6: *Oh no. You can't be a doctor.*

Why not?

Girls can't be doctors because they would look silly if they were doctors.

Well, can't girls help heal people?

Oh yes. They can be nurses, *but not doctors.*

Would you like to fly an airplane?

No.

Why not?

Because boys do that.

Well, would you like to be a scientist?

No-o-o. Girls are sometimes scientists, but I wouldn't want to be one.

How about an astronaut?

No. (Giggle). Boys are astronauts. And, besides, most girls don't wear space suits, do they? And girls can't drive a rocket. They'd be so scared.

How do you know?

I just thought it up myself. Nobody told me.

Some people deny the fact that girls are encouraged to limit their ambitions for achieving in the world. They prefer to cling to the belief that women are inherently incapable of, or ill-suited to, or disinterested in particular kinds of accomplishment: or else that women are as free as men to choose alternatives—whether to go to university, get a job, be a housewife. And superficially it appears that a woman does have this choice; but in most cases the choice has been undermined by experiences that have come before. Dr. Ronald Lambert, a social psychologist at the University of Waterloo, points out: "In many respects the choice has already been foreordained. As a child she had learned some of the important ideas of what it is to be a woman. There is freedom, but freedom in the sense that many of the values by which she will make her choice have already been laid down early in life."

What does your father do?

Cathy, 4: *He works.*

And your mother?

She works too—in the house.

When you grow up would you like to work too, like your dad?

No. Girls can't work like their daddies.

Would you like to do any work when you get older?

Yes. I'd like to work like a mother.

What kinds of work do mothers do?

They clean the dishes, they wash the floors, they wash the clothes, they make the beds, and they make breakfast, they make lunch and they make supper.

How do you know that?

From Sesame Street on T.V.

When you grow up, would you like to do what your mother does or what your father does?

Ron, 7: *What my father does. He's a chemist. And he makes things.*

What does your mother do?

Nothing. She just cleans up the house sometimes.

Do you think she could work if she wanted to?

Yeah. I guess so.

Could she become a chemist like your father?

No. But maybe she could be like—a secretary. But not anything else.

Why not?

You have to be smarter to be a chemist than a secretary. And girls aren't as smart. And she's a girl.

From **Our Favorite Things.** Illustrations © 1968 by BOJE-VERLAG, Stuttgart.

My friends and I love to dress up and look at ourselves in the mirror. We turn this way and that. I think I look best in yellow.

The girls are always inside wasting their time with clothes. My friends like to run around outside. We play catch and Tommy throws the ball highest of anyone. But no matter how high he throws the ball, I always catch it.

Although children's story books may seem innocent and fanciful, they unfortunately perpetuate rigid cultural differences in boys and girls. Professor Lambert states: "There is a self-fulfilling prophecy at work. Women learn that certain activities are appropriate. They learn there is one role appropriate for males, and another for females. And so they conform to that role. Then we turn around and say: 'You see, they really don't achieve as well as men achieve.' In other words we have stacked the deck."

What does your mother do?

Olga, 4: *She gets lots of money from daddy so she buys good things.*
What does your daddy do?
He goes to work.
Would you like to do that when you grow up?
No. I want to be a wife.
How do you feel about your mother and your father?
I like my mother best. Because she's a girl.
If you had one wish, for when you grow up, what would it be?
The only thing I wish is to get married, and I also think I'll have babies and things like that.

Even in play children begin to reveal the effects of strictly defined male-female patterns. Girls are usually encouraged to imitate their mothers and model their activities after such routines as housekeeping, dressing up, childcare. Boys participate in sports and other more impulsive, more spirited activities. Often the differences during early childhood are not so obvious—in many cases boys and girls may play certain games together and girls may use so-called male toys such as trucks and chemistry sets. But eventually girls are urged to drop their tomboy habits and behave in more

John Phillips

"feminine" ways. Whether or not all children accept these tenets without rebellion, the fact remains that such behaviour is expected. Cathy, a fifteen-year-old teenager, describes what it was like as a small girl: "When I was a little girl my mother always said 'Stay in.' She encouraged me to play with dolls, do the dishes, or she would buy me little dusting pans and mops. It was always 'Don't you look pretty.' She wanted me to be a perfect pretty little girl with bows in my hair.

"But my brother, he was encouraged to be rugged. He could ride his bike and get dirty and filthy. My dad used to always take my brother to the stock-car races and I always wanted to go too. They used to sit and talk about cars, or go to watch my dad race. Boys always had more interesting things to do like that. And now many girls are quite ignorant of such matters. Boys will talk about cars; and all the girls do is sit there. They simply don't care about anything at all of interest or importance."

Although imposition of these values is so pervasive that it almost goes unnoticed, it is possible that as children, girls may recognize the signs—that doors are being quietly closed. Unfortunately it is almost impossible for young children to rebel outwardly against their assigned sex roles; yet it is clear that the resentment is there:

What do you think is the difference between boys and girls?

Marlene, 9: *Boys always play hockey, baseball, stuff like that. Girls just sit around. But they could do it too, if they wanted to.*

Carol, 6: *Girls can play house but boys don't want to play house. And they don't have to play house. Boys do things that they want to do.*

Right now you're hugging me and wrapping your arms around me. Does your brother do that to people?

Jane, 5: *No. And if he did the people wouldn't like it. Boys aren't supposed to act cute.*

Boys learn to face crisis early in life through competition, strenuous activity, even fighting. Impelled by their own natural drives and energies, and society's demands that they be independent, boys begin at an early age to develop a sense of self and individual judgment. They are taught to risk impulsivity, aggressiveness, even punishment, despite the attitudes or responses of other people. Boys, in a sense, are taught to defy— taught to please by not always pleasing.

Girls, on the other hand, are discouraged from roughing it, from physical duress or conflict. They are encouraged instead to remain dependent on the will of others. They learn to bend toward others for affirmation and thus lack an early impetus to seek out a stronger sense of self. As Judith Bardwick and Elizabeth Douvan explain in *Woman in Sexist Society*: "Girls' self-esteem remains dependent upon other people's acceptance and love; they continue to use the skills of others instead of evolving their own. The boy begins, before the age of five, to develop a sense of self and criteria of worth which are relatively independent of others' responses."

What kinds of games do you play?

Lisa, 5: *I like to be in play fashion shows and win.*
What do you have to do to win?
I have to be nice and soft and graceful.
Are boys like that too?
No. Boys are mean all the time. They are bullies because they beat up girls.
Do girls play rough back?
No. They should be graceful always.
Why?
Well, if I acted clumsy, people wouldn't like me.

Lisa has learned to avoid being unfeminine because "people wouldn't like me". Although some girls may rebel in one way or another against their conditioning and although many do not fit the barbie-doll mold of sweetness and acquiescence, it is such behaviour that is expected—therefore it is for such behaviour that girls are rewarded. Otherwise, why would a girl's dislike of such stereotyping be termed "rebellion"?

Women are often referred to as being "other-oriented", as opposed to men, who are said to be "self-oriented". These attitudes learned in childhood lead women to continue relying on others for their identity, especially on men. Professor Lambert comments: "Woman is relatively defined—she is defined relative to the man. She is defined in terms of what her husband has done. Thus her self-definition remains fixed relative to someone else."

How do boys fight?

Olga, 4:   *They kick each other a lot. All girls do is hug each other or kiss. And they cry lots of times.*
Why?
Maybe they got hurt, or people don't listen to them, or they don't get what they want—so they cry.

Along with learning a dependent code of behaviour, women also learn to shy away from boldly asserting their ideas or demands. Guided by adults to be agreeable and compliant, little girls learn to act indirectly instead of directly. As Olga illustrates, tactics such as crying become substitutes for overt action. Out of this type of experience comes woman's sometime reputation for devious, scheming behaviour, or alternatively her tendency to react to stress with tears and childlike tantrums.

Are there any differences between boys and girls?

Bob, 7:   *Boys are better. Boys do more things. I'm happy to be a boy because boys become the bosses of the families.*
What do you want to be when you grow up?
Superman.
Why?
So I can dump girls in the lake. Girls are stupid. They can't do many jobs. They are retarded.

What do you want to be when you grow up?

Nancy, 6:   *A princess.*
Why?
Because a princess is pretty and nice.

Denied the opportunity to experiment independently with their personalities, little girls readily respond to meek stereotypes of the feminine ideal, and spend their lifetimes striving to emulate them. As reality intrudes— a bullying little boy, sexual frustration, depressing housework, female competition—women often retreat even further into fantasy.

Fantasy can be a natural and beautiful aspect of childhood, but if used as an escape, as so often happens with women, it becomes an excuse for avoiding action. Many housewives become compulsive television-comedy fans or become absorbed by the glamorous events of other people's lives or by some impossible idealized future of their own. And rather than summoning up

John Phillips

Laura Jones

courage to get out of depressing environments, women tend to blame themselves for not being able to adapt or live up to the ideal. They learn to look for deficiencies within themselves, rather than reforming the situation.

Acceptance of the feminine mystique also encourages girls to believe that they must be, or deserve to be, protected from harsh reality. Maturity is necessary only for males; females can be allowed to avoid it by relying on a man. "Supporting yourself is hard. Don't risk a career. Get a man", girls are advised. Ambitions are satisfied indirectly, vicariously.

But just as girls are denied an entire realm of cultural and emotional experience due to their femaleness, so are boys denied a wide range of feelings because of their maleness. They are whisked very quickly out of the poetic beauty of childhood and imagination into the world of concrete activity. Those men who do lean towards more creative, imaginative pursuits are often labelled "effeminate", in the same discriminatory fashion that women who enjoy activity or competition are labelled "masculine" or "ball-busters". A wide spectrum of feeling is denied men—release through crying, admission of weakness.

Some men are beginning to realize that they too are trapped—by the masculine mystique. Says Ron Lambert: "The problems of man's virility should be included in discussions on feminism. The other side of this picture, too often ignored, are the problems that men themselves feel—men who are required to show initiative, move ahead, be competent in a work sense and yet who may not feel really up to it. They can become guilty and feel incompetent because they cannot succeed in specific male areas.

"When males are socialized to be competitive, they are also taught not to cry. In so doing they are denying an important part of their expression. They are being taught not to be sensitive towards other people, not to relate in a personal way to others.

"Presumably if the feminist movement is to get anywhere, it will have to involve also the liberation of men from very traditional ways of thinking about what a man must necessarily do, think or feel to be a man. Obviously, men too pay a price.

"The issue of war is closely related to the problem of feminism in this perhaps perverse way. We teach our children to relate in traditional ways. We teach our daughters to relate in an intimate way to others, to be sensitive to other people. Simultaneously, we teach young boys to do those things which are virile, manly, we teach them not to show their feelings, to be concerned with saving face.

"I think in many ways we have deprived boys of a psychological defense against the demands of the state upon them. There is nothing more damning than calling a drafted man a coward. Thus one of the first objections raised against draft resisters or deserters is that they are cowards, they have copped out. Any men who refuse to leave the armed forces usually base their decision on not wanting to appear cowardly. Their traditional conception of the sex roles has taught them to feel the necessity to apologize for any attempt to save their own lives, let alone the lives of other people. In other words, traditional ways of thinking about the sexes are very much involved in maintaining a state of mind, a sense of legitimacy which allows the state now to demand of men traditionally virile behaviour.

"I don't want to oversimplify. There are other factors operating which get us into wars. But I think the significance here is that this is an important psychological element which at least conditions and prepares people for these kinds of demands; as women are liberated so too are their sons liberated."

But although it is crucial that we decide to rid ourselves of the present mode of socialization, the problem remains of finding alternatives. How to raise children free of sex-role stereotyping? The problem is not easily answered, as explained by Judy LaMarsh, a serious feminist, lawyer, author and former Canadian cabinet minister.

If I were to have a girl child right now, I don't know if I would have the strength of my own convictions to bring her up as a person. Perhaps she would be happier, free of her role. Then too she might be very unhappy, for as a child growing up she would hit so many of the taboos in the world. So perhaps not socializing her in a traditional manner would be a dreadful thing to do.

I would still be more likely to put the frilly clothes on her, still teach her to cry, let it out, still teach her all the things that I was taught and all my sisters were taught thousands of years before me; because I don't really know what happens when you teach a child otherwise.

The main point is the necessity to allow girls (and boys) to grow up developing their own independent personalities. Frilly feminine clothes and soft manners are not harmful in themselves but in what they represent—a submissive, shy, unconfident personality, or else a devious one. Girls will have to be encouraged to fulfill their ambitions positively and directly. But that's not easy. Whatever lack of confidence girls experience in childhood is only reinforced in adolescence. On the following pages we have included excerpts from a discussion we taped with several articulate high-school students, about how their early socialization patterns have continued to develop.

Mark, 19: *Aggressiveness is when a girl has her own ideas, ideas which are not like a pat set feminine formula. That sort of girl turns off a lot of guys. If she is an individual, not just one of the group, but an individual that you can clearly identify as one, then I think many guys would get turned off because they wouldn't know how to handle her. They would not know how to handle a girl whose reactions are not set, who would not react in a predictable manner they could anticipate.*

At a time of life when both males and females are under great stress socially and physically, a teenage girl copes with the extra burden of defining herself as a female as well as a person. Not only must she adjust to her physical femininity, but she must also develop the appropriate mental femininity as laid down by the culture. The adolescent girl is constantly aware of her need to behave in a "feminine" manner and to be attractive to boys. But femininity is a rather ambiguous state.

Bardwick and Douvan explain: "For the girl overt freedoms, combined with cultural ambiguity, result in an unclear image of femininity. As a result of vagueness about how to become feminine or even what is feminine, the girl responds to the single clear directive—she withdraws from what is clearly masculine."

© 1970 National Periodical Publications, Inc.

Diane, 16: *Girls are afraid of being labelled as aggressive. I definitely know that I am. Boys do the asking and that's the way it is. You comply, or else you lose your femininity. It's just not the proper thing to do—to be aggressive. The guy is supposed to do all the suggesting and you must sit back and wait for it. I don't like the idea at all because I'm impatient about sitting around for a guy. But I won't go and ask a guy out first. However, there are lots of ways of getting around that.*

Aggressiveness in girls is definitely unacceptable. The code of femininity demands that girls use more oblique methods to attain their desires. Earlier in this chapter we heard a little girl say that crying was such a tool. Above, Diane talks of "ways of getting around" the cardinal rule of waiting for the boy to make the first move. Freud calls this "the active pursuit of a passive function". An example of such a "passive function":

How to Date A Teen-Age Boy
You should make the first move with a boy. You should take the initiative, in showing interest. You should arrange conversations . . . but you must stop short of actually suggesting that the two of you go out together. When you do this you are no longer really feminine. You are crossing the line into male territory.

> *Ellen Peck*
> How to Get A Teen-Age Boy and
> What to Do With Him When You Get Him

(This book sold over 50,000 copies in hardcover during 1969 and according to a major Toronto bookseller was bought mainly by mothers for their daughters.)

A girl's search for femininity also sets up a conflict between intellectual success and social popularity. Many girls find themselves in the contradictory situation of actually fearing academic achievement—and therefore compromise themselves by playing down their abilities in order to avoid intimidating the boys.

How to Seem Less Intelligent
A girl who shows too much intellect and argues down her dates is forgetting a guy's insecurity. Keep it in mind. When guys grow up, they stop being bothered by the fact that women can often talk and write (and think?) more fluidly and quickly. They accept the fact. They use it. They hire the brightest gals they can find to type their letters and correct their mistakes. But that doesn't mean you can correct Dan's pronunciation now.

> *Ellen Peck*
> How to Get A Teen-Age Boy and
> What to Do With Him When You Get Him

Advice such as the above may cause some girls to react in the opposite way—repress their desire to be liked by men rather than deny their abilities. In either case, an unnatural choice is set up. For most teenage girls, the overriding obsession is to be always feminine. And to be feminine is to be linked with a man. The pressure to conform to the expectations of others, begun early in childhood, continues into adolescence— the "others" this time being men. Immediately a conflict occurs between intellectual success and social success, which later may become a conflict between choosing a career or marriage.

Susan, 16: *If I did meet a guy who really thought that a girl's place was in the home and all that stuff, and if the guy really loved me and wouldn't be happy any other way—then if I wanted to marry him I should think I'd have to give up the career. In my case such a sacrifice would depend on how fascinating the man is.*

Reprinted through courtesy of **Love Diary** Comic Magazine.

Diane, 16: *You have to be involved in something. I really believe that. But if you intend putting in a lot of time in working towards a career, you have to consider if that is worth all the trouble in the long run, for a girl. Because if you do get married, can you carry it on? In many cases, I guess you could not.*

During adolescence the pressure on a girl to find a boy she can depend on can become so great that she fears never finding one. Although marriage or a love relationship may not be an immediate goal, the fear that it may not happen is ever present.

Diane, 16: *I think that a lot of women have made sacrifices in order to be married. The woman is in the position of fearing whether she will ever find a man. She may be very afraid of never finding anyone; so in that case I am sure she would take a husband rather than a job if and when he came along. She would give up her career or studies thinking she could probably continue them some other time; but the chances of getting a husband some other time might be less.*

Women who challenge the need to make such a ridiculous choice may be handed what is, in the true sense of the words, an old wives' tale—the advice that settling for less, for mediocrity, is better than nothing at all.

Ron, 17: *It is much easier for a boy to set his expectations high. A girl has to be extremely determined to do what she desires in order to succeed. Because she is constantly being told by everybody: "Let the boy do it. Marry one."*

For adolescent boys the compulsion to find a member of the opposite sex simply does not exist to the degree that it does in girls. Even in adolescence the difference in male and female priorities is clearly defined.

Ron, 17: *Right now I can't consider my thoughts of family or marriage because at the moment the idea of marriage is so far removed from my mind. It seems such a remote idea—me ever getting married.*

Cathy, 15: *My brother has two important things—his music and his girlfriend. Sometimes the music comes first. And I think that with most men, their careers come first. They work all the time and they just do not think about their wives, as much as their wives think about them. Their wives are just there and they feed them.*

For girls adolescence is beset by all kinds of restrictions on self-expression. Constantly forced to be aware of the attitudes of boys, many teenage girls become super-self-conscious. Their sense of self becomes based on how they see other people seeing them, a potentially neurotic situation. Individuality is a liability.

Let's get rid of that "Be Yourself" myth. People keep parroting "Be Yourself" as if this were a magic formula. What is this precious self, anyway? . . . Do you really want to be a sixteen-year-old fossil? . . .

What attitude are you projecting? . . . The I'm great attitude is terrific for the corridors on the first floor and for the world at large, and you never lose it; but—what are the boys like in this class? Even more specifically, what is Greg like?

Is Greg the intellectual type and fascinated by geography? Then, you're going to have to look at least interested in it. Your attitude is, "I'm great; thoughtful, too." If Greg, though, is the comic or activities major, busy planning for after class and indifferent to mean annual rainfalls, your attitude is, "I'm great. Casual about this class, but great."

> *Ellen Peck*
> How to Get A Teen-Age Boy and
> What to Do With Him When You Get Him

Many people refuse to accept the fact that such a process really goes on—that women are deliberately discouraged from pursuing a wide range of skills and means of self-expression. Instead they prefer to point out that many women do attend university, graduate and enter careers. And this is true. But it is also true that women tend to choose careers that are decidedly "female" in nature—teaching, social work, nursing.

This is partly a result of the mode of socialization most girls receive. As was shown early in this chapter, little girls are encouraged to adopt other-oriented, other-pleasing skills and attitudes; during adolescence the pursuit of femininity draws women away from certain intellectual and "male" ventures. According to Bardwick and Douvan (*Women in Sexist Society*), this causes many women to develop interpersonal skills as opposed to professional skills—to rely on being good for, or pleasing to, others, through their personal qualities instead of achieving by individual projects or talents. Consequently women deliberately withdraw from independence; and the effects of that withdrawal can be extremely frustrating and dissatisfying.

Reprinted through courtesy of **Love Diary** Comic Magazine.

Ambivalence is clearly seen in the simultaneous enjoyment of one's feminine identity, qualities, goals and achievement, and the perception of them as less important, meaningful, or satisfying than those of men. Girls envy boys; boys do not envy girls.

Judith Bardwick and Elizabeth Douvan
Women in Sexist Society

Susan, 16: *Boys are more interesting to talk to than girls. Girls tend to be more emotional perhaps. What bothers me most about girl-talk is that it invariably centres around guys, dating experiences—this sort of social atmosphere. Whereas with guys, you can talk about more interesting things.*

Paul, 17: *To be quite honest it has been my experience that if I am sitting talking to another guy about something very important, a girl will suddenly jump in all cute-like with some silly, totally irrelevant comment—like about her grandmother being sick. Also when a girl argues and you ask her to explain why, give her reasons for a certain opinion, she usually replies: "I don't know."*

Mark, 19: *Because I am a boy I know I can do a lot more things and get away with them. I know if I were a girl and did some of the things I did in high school a lot more trouble would have occurred. I've sworn in school and nothing serious happened. If a girl had sworn, the situation would have been much worse.*

Diane, 16: *Guys are encouraged to behave differently than girls. I find they do a lot of stupid, crazy things. I enjoy making fun of them. But sometimes I wish I were a guy —and able to do just crazy things—wild things!*

At the suggestion that we change our present patterns of socialization, many people conjure up nightmare visions of a time when all differences between the sexes will be obliterated. But it is important to keep in mind that the sexes now are taught to conform to very rigid forms of behaviour—individual traits of character are subordinate to the sex-roles. In attempting to free children of strict male-female conditioning, we would really be freeing men and women to try out a richer diversity of life patterns.

Will you want to marry when you grow up?

Ron, 7: *Yes.*

And what would you do as the husband?

I would work and my mother would do the cooking.

Your mother?

I mean the girl I marry.

Couldn't she work too?

No.

Why not?

Because, just because.

There must be a reason.

No. There's no reason.

What would you do if the girl you marry refused to stay home and wanted to work?

Well—then I guess we would both go to work and we'd lock the house.

Laura Jones

The body is a woman's own environment.

Vogue, *April, 1971*

Fashion

A wealthy woman postures before a mirror in a store's elegant salon. She gazes intently at the reflection, inspects the form and the body from every vantage point, imagines she is someone else watching the image. Her face is tight, her eyes are tense. Her decision, she knows, is a test of her worth. She is shopping for clothes.

Downtown a young girl flits through the racks in a crowded boutique. The room is hot, she is tired, but her search goes on. She quickly tries on garment after garment in a small, close changing room, jostles for position before a large mirror. She is surrounded by thin, smiling, nodding sales people. She must be sure. Her decision is crucial.

What are these women looking for? Why the intensity, the religious scrutiny? What is driving these women is the power of what they are promised. Physical imagery. Self-expression. Definition through fashion.

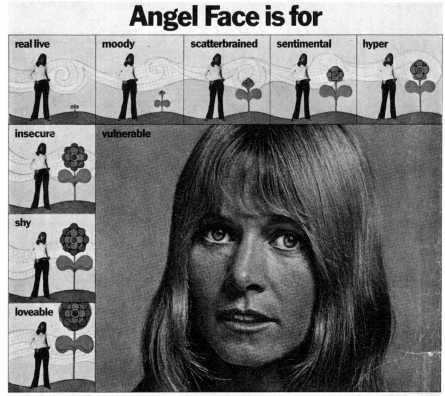

Not all women take part in this fashion ritual. The countercultural community is establishing a carefree, less demanding concept of dress that avant-garde designers like Rudi Gernreich look to for inspiration and hail as a symbol of a new universal in human relations. According to Gernreich, the so-called glamour magazines like *Vogue* are beginning to die: "All the old social structures are rapidly changing—snobbism, the select few—we now detest these characteristics, and that symbolism in fashion is fading. The glamour magazines are in trouble; financially speaking, they are not what they used to be."

The secret is freedom and that means no bras or girdles. You got to do what you want to do and wear what you want to wear. Everybody is so hung up on the matching game—the shoes have to match the bag which matches the coat and dress. But the big question is, is it matching your soul.

Janis Joplin
Village Voice

Although the clothing-as-freedom concept is gaining acceptance, the strict dictates of glamour still hold sway over most women. "Beauty is the foundation of woman's confidence," reads the first line in the brochure for Toronto's Eleanor Fulcher Self-Improvement and Model School. The brochure underlines quite clearly the fact that a woman's first duty is to seek a visual identity. For some women this becomes one interesting facet of their lives. For others it becomes their only attempt at self-expression. Certainly the cult of physical beauty is the most visible manifestation of the feminine need to please others.

Especially to the housewife, the pursuit of fashion is held out as a respectable substitute for more creative types of achievement. For working women who may perform boring tasks daily, clothes can appear to be a release from frustration. In "Fashism", an excellent article from the University of Toronto's undergraduate paper *The Varsity,* writer Susan Perly says: "Women have to exist through the false illusion of fashion, if there is nothing else in their lives they can grasp.... So they attempt to fill the void in their existence by consuming, among other things, clothes. Days are spent searching out the right dress, shoes, stockings, to go with a coat. They see themselves defined through the clothes and accessories they wear. It is their individual statement."

In North America during 1970, women showed their faith in the god of fashion to the tune of $12 billion, all in return for the promise of being in style. To probe

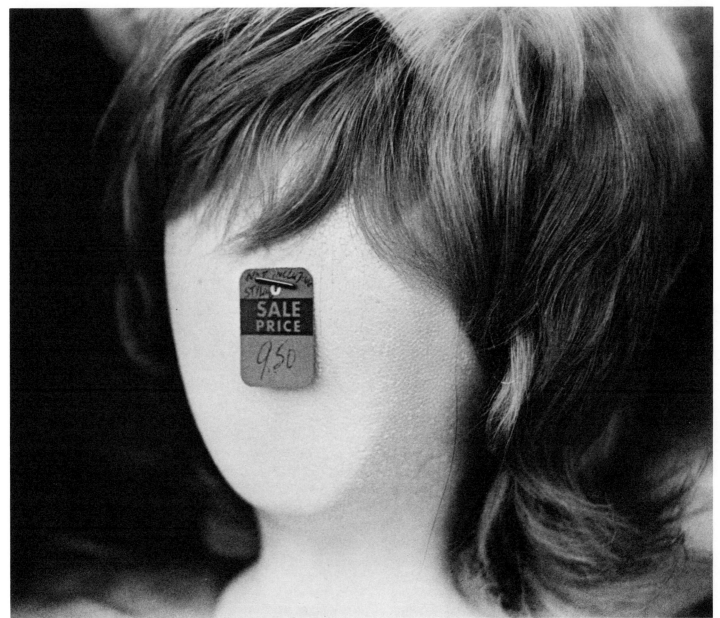

Laura Jones

the psychology behind woman's preoccupation with fashion, we taped original interviews with Montreal couturier John Warden and American "unisex" designer Rudi Gernreich, and a conversation with three Canadian women—sculptor and new feminist Maryonn Kantaroff, boutique designer and former fashion writer for the Toronto *Telegram* Marni Grobba, and Heather Petrie, a twenty-two-year-old secretary and former model.

Maryonn Kantaroff: *Women are confident today according to how society views them. Their confidence is due to their appearance, not their achievement, or personality.*

Heather Petrie: *As a former model, I found the stress on beauty to be destructive. I began to believe the girl in the mirror was real, but she wasn't. Make-up is just not real. With hair pieces and all those props I tended to get myself confused with that mirror image, or the photograph in the magazine. And then, when I was without the props, I felt nervous and suffered a great lack of confidence.*

There was a time when I had to put my eyelashes on to go to the laundromat. I really began to lose myself behind that whole veneer of make-up. It was definitely destructive. Especially if one's personality is unformed, because then it takes that much longer to define who you are. You have all that getting in the way.

As far as cosmetics are used for adornment in a conscious and creative way, they are not emblems of inauthenticity; it is when they are presented as the real thing, . . . that their function is deeply suspect. The women who dare not go out without their false eyelashes are in serious psychic trouble.

> *Germaine Greer*
> The Female Eunuch

Heather Petrie: *Make-up is not designed to change you at all; it is designed to relate to the glamour-magazine image which says everyone must have high cheek bones and slender noses. And people forget that the most beautiful faces are the character faces. As far as attractiveness goes, that all gets lost somewhere. You end up looking like all the models look, like they came off an assembly line.*

I honestly believe we must reach the point where our confidence has nothing to do with the way we look. Women who tend to feel better when they are dressed up, as opposed to just being comfortable, are insecure.

Insecurity is a theme delicately played upon by the fashion industry; it is not, as some would believe, created by the industry only. As long as woman remains society's embodiment of human beauty and sexuality, as long as the onus is upon her, and not the male, to be stylish and alluring, and as long as she remains frustrated by not achieving creatively in other ways, woman will be insecure in regard to her physical appearance.

But according to Montreal fashion designer John Warden, insecurity is the prologue to beauty. He told us: "You certainly have to be insecure to look good. You cannot look great if you are not insecure about yourself. If you are sure, you would not try harder. It is this drive to improve that creates beauty. Confident women are passed by in the street by people who remark only lightly, 'That's just another pretty face.' Everyone in this industry is complex, insecure, whatever. It is a terrible dynamic, but it is necessary. Their insecurity creates an excitement that really provokes a lot of things to happen. To really stand out you must be a little paranoid."

Rudi Gernreich doesn't agree. He feels the days of fashion-magazine insecurity-baiting ploys are over: "If a woman is relaxed about beauty and doesn't have to compete, she comes off looking better. She no longer has to be beautiful and in a sense therefore becomes more beautiful. She cannot be beautiful if she *has* to, if it is imposed. That is why some older women are such pathetic, monstrous creatures. They have to be beautiful until death. Our concept of beauty is changing, kids no longer attach so much importance to stereotyped form. All this traditional cultural symbolism is going out. The number of women that still need the traditional kind of support is diminishing. They are immature."

Last year Jackie Kennedy Onassis spent $300,000 on clothes. That is, admittedly, an astronomical figure. More down to earth, no doubt, is the advice of *Harper's Bazaar* fashion columnist Eugenia Sheppard, who suggests: "The absolute minimum for which a fastidious woman of fashion can cover her nakedness" is $20,000. "A really clothes-conscious aspirant," she adds, "will spend upward of $100,000 a year on dresses alone."

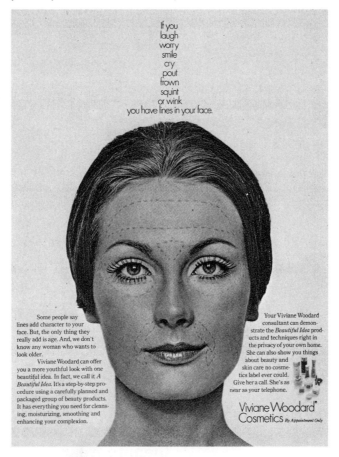

Cosmetics and dress are created to erase, so far as possible, the pattern of living on a woman's face.

Katherine Aanspach
The Why of Fashion

Today cosmetic surgery is accepted as a natural extension of a woman's toilette. A *Toronto Star* story of May 26, 1971, reported that most women seeking breast augmentation (mammaplasty) were not young girls or topless dancers "but housewives with several children who have been self-conscious about a small bustline for years". Through expensive and painful operations, cosmetic surgery can now redesign almost anything—sagging derrières, thigh bulge, drooping stomachs or the jawline. The latter is called facial architecture, the aesthetic arm of dentistry. Only flabby arms cannot be refitted, says Brazilian beauty surgeon Dr. Ivo Putanguy, "because there's no way of hiding the scars". So pity the flabby-armed hordes; for them there is no salvation. . . .

Why do women go to such extremes, why have they become so obsessed with being beautiful? Feeling good and looking good, even physical adornment, are healthy, natural aims. Using apparel as a vehicle to extend one's identity visually is enjoyable. There is drama and enchantment in dressing up. After all, life is partly theatre, or as Ken Kesey says, in Tom Wolfe's *The Electric Kool-Aid Acid Test*, "Everybody, everybody everywhere has his own movie going." Turning on with clothes can be fun. But being *obsessed* by beauty and wardrobe is not fun; it suggests a dangerous narcissism, desperation, and a tremendous output of energy that may be more satisfyingly applied elsewhere.

Marni Grobba: *Fashion is an expression or outlet for a lot of people who cannot paint or perform some other kind of creative activity.*
Maryonn Kantaroff: *I think that is a spurious argument.*
Marni Grobba: *I believe it though. I really do.*
Maryonn Kantaroff: *It must make it easier to work in the fashion field if you believe it, but it is a spurious argument. There is no way that fashion as it is sold is helping anyone's creativity. On the contrary—satisfaction comes from pulling something out of oneself rather than buying it. If it comes down to a question of "Do I choose this" or "Do I choose that," one spends the whole day looking for some kind of choice, as opposed to creating it by oneself.*

Women should wear what their men want them to wear.

Ann-Margret
Vogue, June 1971

Maryonn Kantaroff: *Ultimately a woman dresses to please a man because getting a man is a woman's prime motive. Her status in life comes not from herself, but from the man with whom she associates. And so women grow up with the feeling that to obtain a male they must compete, and compete on the worst possible level —their physicalness. During adolescence it is very destructive. Who has the nicest legs, who develops their breasts first, whose hair is longest and blondest. Whereas boys, while growing up, compete on a different level—who can run the fastest, who gets the best marks at school, who is toughest. They can fight it out. To me that is much healthier kind of competition. Women, instead, learn to compete destructively and to suspect one another. Women really do put down other women.*

We speak of their dressing for men; they are actually doing so only indirectly. At a party, for example, a woman's first concern is to sum up the competition. She does not waste her time watching men, the reason being very clear—a woman cannot choose a man. She is in the position of object *who must appeal to someone else.*

Marni Grobba: *I see this trait in men now—even men who are forty and fifty are taking on this motivation. Dressing in competition with each other for a lady, and I don't like it. They do not appeal to me in this manner at all.*

Maryonn Kantaroff: *That is understandable since the industry has suddenly woken up and realized that the other half—the male world—is an unexploited market. But the interesting thing is that you should find it disturbing in men but not women.*

Heather Petrie: *Women also work hard at not just looking good, but looking better than "her". And the saddest point about this is that it is reinforced by everything from year one—the little girl on the street with her mother is complimented by some dear old lady who says, "Isn't she pretty." That's how it starts and from then on it gets worse. She becomes fourteen and gangly, with nothing there and too much here and she's reading glamour magazines. It's just a vicious game. The whole scene in fashion magazines is deliberately casual—sea fronts with rocks, surf and the inevitable handsome man. What the reader doesn't realize is that she is wearing four hair-pieces and the guy is probably a homosexual who is going home to his young man friend. It really makes me angry because there are teenagers who believe in this.*

But that is also an extension of how the mother would wish to see her daughter. The whole fashion thing is extremely exploitative for women. It keeps them consuming instead of producing, by attacking their insecurity. The fashion industry makes you feel that there is something wrong with you all the time and they use this to get to your head.

Women are insecure and need someone to tell them what to wear.
> *William Frohman*
> *Toronto garment manufacturer*

Heather Petrie: *I think the fashion industry is responsible for a lot of mixed-up people, especially older women. A woman of forty is beginning to feel very insecure. And I believe the fashion industry is the villain. I have to.*

Marni Grobba: *You cannot put fashion strictly in the role of villain. Whether fashion-change just for the sake of it is valid or not, it motivates women to purchase new clothes every year. If we produced the same styles year-in, year-out, an invaluable industry would die. And think how boring we would look. Fashion is variety. If you want to buy a very butch-looking longer length, tailored or military look, you can; if you want to go Victorian you can; it's all what mood you want to put on.*

Maryonn Kantaroff: *I don't think it is mood we are really speaking of; it is "What will I be today." We are being urged to be a Gaucho on Tuesday and a Gypsy on Wednesday.*

Marni Grobba: *What's wrong with that?*

Heather Petrie: *That's bad because if you do it too often you forget who you are.*

Maryonn Kantaroff: *Some people don't know who they are and I think fashion well and truly keeps them from finding out.*

A woman's constant awareness of how she is being seen can become a neurotic symptom. She may quickly confuse her outward appearance (her "mythical" self) with her real self, and as Heather explained further back, may consequently lose her sense of identity altogether.

The "split-personality" ad is no joke. Even intelligence is being pushed as a costume gambit, as another super, sought-after addition to a woman's wardrobe. "The look of awareness" is touted as "the most fashionable look of all" in *The National Observer* ad on the following page. Women are being encouraged to climb onto a carousel of swiftly changing identities—all in order to construct a mythical variety of images for the favourable response of others.

. . . when one discusses the impaired sensuousness of American women one refers it . . . to the gap that all Americans face when the actual sensuous experience must be adjusted to the visual ideal that is held up before them.

Margaret Mead
Male and Female

This gap between a woman's self and the visual image she presents creates sensual and sexual problems. A woman in bed may still be constantly aware of her image, or her image in relation to other female images that she has seen idealized in magazines or films. Again a distance is created between a woman, her body, and the man she is with.

For some women, classic beauty is not always considered a boon. The luxury of "looking good" comes at a high price in toil, conspicuousness and self-consciousness. Not all women wish to be noticed, visually outstanding. One extremely attractive woman interviewed talked about the relief of the anonymity she experienced during a period when she had a serious skin condition: "I would walk down the street and not have to worry about other people looking at me; they weren't. In fact men were visibly rejecting me, but instead of feeling hurt I was laughing inside, feeling a great sense of privacy and freedom. I could spend my time thinking of other things and my energy did not have to be wasted in concern for cultivating an image for the sake of people with whom I would have no contact anyway."

In his book *They Became What They Beheld*, Edmund Carpenter talks of the advantage of the anonymity of ugliness, the advantage of being "unspecified" by appearance: "Cosmetics and clothing advertisers assume everybody wants to be beautiful. Actually, lots don't. Being beautiful is being specified. A beautiful woman is expected to 'dress and act accordingly'— that is, to fill a defined, restricted part. It's a challenge, of sorts, which not everyone is willing, or interested, in meeting."

As our culture moves from stricture to relaxation, so move the relations between men and women. Rudi Gernreich speaks with assurance about the present emancipation of women, and men, as symbolized by dress. Fashion, he says, has become old-fashioned; and so have many other forms of social relations: "Fashion has become anti-fashion. It stands for values which no longer apply to our current thinking. All the male-female symbolism is beginning to fade. I no longer think in male-female terms in design. We are moving into an era of less conspicuous, more anonymous clothes. There is a coming together of male and female, and men are no longer looking at women in the old way because they too are being looked at. This statement of unisex says: 'We're human beings—not males and females.' This is a social statement, not a sexual one. And sexually, it is healthier.

"In films the pedestal, stereotyped image of the 'star' no longer exists. I see a much more uniform look between both sexes which now allows us to individualize ourselves in other ways. In the future, the individuality of a person will manifest itself in different ways. By wearing like clothes, people will be urged to probe further into each others' characters.

"Unisex clothing will help to bring out the real, deeper differences by doing away with the superficial differences of sexual differentiation, which simply get in the way of understanding.

"Historically, woman reverted to slavery—owned by a man so she had to be beautiful, a desirable object to be owned. But now she does not have to be a slave. A complete revolution of women's emancipation has taken place in the last decade. But many women are afraid to be free—it requires a certain responsibility to be a creative and active participant."

Fine little girl she waits for me
she's as plastic as she can be
she paints her face with plastic goo
and wrecks her hair with some shampoo.
Plastic people, hey baby, you're such a drag.

Frank Zappa
of The Mothers of Invention

Sexuality

The most commonly heard put-down of feminists is "All they need is a good fuck," to which most women react with anger and become indignant or speechless. This accusation is the worst of all because often, though by no means always, it hits its mark. Until finally women have begun to answer, "Damn right we're frustrated—and we know why." One of the first things to start cropping up at consciousness-raising sessions—the thing rarely admitted aloud before—is that women have plenty of sexual hang-ups; after the sexual revolution, frigidity simply went underground.

In addition to its other aims, women's liberation seeks the liberation of female sexuality. If power relationships between men and women are unbalanced in favour of the male, there's no place where it is more obvious and more painful than in their most intimate relations.

For this chapter we taped two rather candid discussions on sex, one with an all-male group (no women were present, although the men were aware that we would listen to the tapes later); and one with an all-female group. Obviously the two groups are not scientifically valid cross-sections of society, and so the wider significance of their statements about sex must be judged personally by the reader.

Although the people in both groups were originally of varied backgrounds, nationalities and classes, they can all now be considered middle-class Canadians.

The women range in age from twenty-three to thirty-two. Ellen, Linda and Nicole are married and have careers. Cathy is married, has two children and just recently returned to work. Gloria is single and teaches high school. Amy has been divorced, now lives with another man, and also works.

The men are four professionals between twenty-four and thirty-five. Bruce, Chris and Paul are married. Stefan is still a bachelor.

The difference in the tone of these discussions on tape is so remarkable that the contrast alone is enough to make you understand sexual politics on a private level, simply by imagining these men and women paired up with each other. To be perfectly honest, we were rather amazed to find that the men's attitudes fit so easily the male-chauvinist stereotype, and that the women's experience accurately reflects the feminist assertion that women are oppressed in the bedroom.

We know that many men and women have been able
to transcend this situation; but they are, probably,
exceptional.

The women, while occasionally humorous about sex,
have a largely problematical approach to it, a great
respect for it, and see the sexual experience primarily
as one of communication. Now, although none of the
women admits to never having had an orgasm, from
the discussion it would appear that some have not; they
either feel they have to save face, or, not knowing
exactly what an orgasm is, cannot be sure they haven't
and may have mistaken strong arousal for climax. They
also seem glad of the chance to get some of these
things out in the open and to find that they are not as
abnormal or as different as they had feared.

Listening to the tape of the men is an entirely different experience. They are raucous and loud and gross
and grotesquely funny—and depressing. The emotional
emptiness of the sexual experience for them is expressed by one when he says: "It's a pretty good thing
but it's one hell of a letdown when you're finished."
An indication of the pressures they feel during the sex
act is their description of their role as a "performance".
Often they have difficulty keeping on topic, being irre-
sistibly drawn to talking about business and money.
(These parts of the tape have been edited out.) At one
point, the man who is making the tape for us an-
nounces into the microphone: "Sorry girls, this is way
off topic but business is also part of a man's life."
In fact life seems to them largely a question of getting
"a piece of the action"—and that expression refers to
both money and women. The subject-object relationship
between men and women has never seemed so clear.
Their adolescence was spent "grabbing" for "tits" and
"cunts" of "broads" who, no doubt, like the women
we taped, were suppressing their sexual feelings not
so much to preserve their reputations as their personal
dignity.

Reprinted through courtesy of **Love and Romance** Comic Magazine.

Boys and girls operate on different wavelengths. She has the romantic image of love as it is portrayed in the movies. She envisions the boy as her knight in shining armor. He will protect her, stand by her, cherish her. Sexual intercourse will bind them together forever. This is love.

The boy is thinking too—but not about love. Most boys are thinking about making out. Boys make out for a variety of reasons, most usually because it is easier to find a girl who will say yes than to control their physical urges. . . . Many boys make out to prove their manhood. And some boys make out because they want to brag to their peers.

Whether you are going to be a Hold-Out or a Put-Out is your decision. . . . Think it over. It could be the most important decision of your life.

Ann Landers
Truth Is a Stranger

Nicole: *When I was an adolescent my mother was always dropping these vague hints. Like when I went out on a date she'd always say: "Now you be careful, do you hear."*

Once, on New Year's Eve, I went out with a guy who was a few years older than me. He took me to a very nice place, the poshest night club in Vancouver, and it cost him about twenty dollars. A lot of money for a kid in school at that time. Well, my parents didn't want to let me go because, as they saw it, if a boy spends that much money on you it's because he wants something in return.

So I grew up with all these vague fears. I thought everybody was going to attack me. I was brought up to believe that my body was so precious, so much in demand, that I had to protect myself all the time—had to be lashing out all the time.

And it was due to this guy that I went with for a long time—and the long, long conversations we would have —that I got rid of this. He made me see myself as just an ordinary person whose body is no more in demand than the next person's body. And I didn't have to go to extraordinary lengths to protect it.

Ellen: *Until the time I was about eighteen my friends and I had to tread a very fine path between being experienced in some things and not being experienced in others. I remember I was once discussing a date with my girlfriend and she said: "What did you do?" And I told her we kissed or we necked or something, and she said: "Well, you know Ellen, you really shouldn't let boys do that to you. That's really bad. They never do that to me. I don't think they have respect for you."*

It wasn't even what we did, *it was just that they* wanted *to go beyond kissing with me. That alone was bad. So I felt maybe there was something wrong with me. I wasn't being sweet enough or cute enough. I was being too forward, or too much . . .*

Amy: *Too loose. . . .*

Ellen: *. . . that somehow I must appear differently to boys than other girls did.*

Bruce: *In high school I saw girls as something nice to put your arms around and yet you were terribly afraid because you didn't know what to do. You were excited as hell to go out with them and when you finally did— goddamn it, you didn't know what to do with them.*

Chris: *Remember the first time you put your hand on a tit? Right? And immediately you got a hard-on.*

Paul: *The big question was when was the right time to do it. It had to be the proper moment. You didn't want to fluff it. So it was usually before taking them home. And if you saw they had a good time you knew they'd probably do it.*

Chris: *The thing was to get them relatively secluded where they felt at ease, safe. Where no one could* see *them, because they were always worried about this. And then you'd blow it. You'd grab her tit too fast or grab her cunt and that would blow the whole deal.*

When I was about seventeen I developed the left-handed twist, where the broad comes right around in one motion and they never knew what the hell hit them. Then you can grab the tits and play around with them. Then you can try and grab for the cunt.

Stefan: *You always wondered if they felt something when you grabbed their tits. You never knew. . . .*

Bruce: *Nothing pissed you off as much as when you did it and they yawned.*

But I found the best thing was to get on the side of the parents and then take their *daughter out with* their *car. I think that was the high point of my high school love life. And, if you were real suave, you could get the broad who you just screwed to pay for your gasoline.*

[Men] go to great pains to avoid talking about women in front of them ("Not in front of a lady")—it would give their game away. To overhear a bull session is traumatic to a woman: So, all this time she has been considered only "ass," "meat," "twat," or "stuff," to be gotten a "piece of," "that bitch," or "this broad" to be tricked out of money or sex or love! To understand finally that she is no better than other women but completely indistinguishable comes not just as a blow but as total annihilation.

Shulamith Firestone
The Dialectic of Sex

Linda: *I had very strong sexual feelings when I was twelve or thirteen. I would read sexy books and really get all horny. At twelve I started going out with guys, and one of the first times I ever made out with a guy he put his tongue in my mouth and I had no idea what it was all about. I thought it was an uncontrollable reflex because he was so excited. My girlfriends and I would go to the park or swimming and pick up older guys that we didn't know and we would make out with them because I was really digging the physical sensations. But I would have been humiliated to see one of them in another situation. We didn't want to see them again because we would have died if anyone we knew had found out what we were doing.*

But I never went "all the way". One day I went to a drive-in movie with a guy who was much older and had a car. I was thirteen, I think. And he tried to have intercourse with me. I was terrified. I thought losing my virginity would be the end of the world.

Anyway, I went on like this until one day when I was almost fifteen someone told me about a girl at school who was part of the little ruling clique. Apparently she could go out with a guy five or six times and never even kiss him goodnight. So I began to catch on. The more you got from a guy—movies, dinner, etc.—while giving him the least amount of sex in return, the more valuable you were. So for years the farthest I would go was to kiss. But that's when I learned to masturbate. I was having orgasms in my room alone at home and acting the prude when I went out. But for years I was very guilty about what I had done from twelve to fourteen and I lived in constant fear of someone finding out.

Gloria: *I went through five years of high school without getting into any heavy petting or anything. And it was always other girls who were doing that stuff. And you sort of looked on it like, wow, it must be exciting because it's bad and all your friends say it's bad and your mother says it's bad, yet there was something very appealing about it. On the other hand, there was no way that girl could become your friend. I remember one particular girl who got pregnant and no one would talk to her. She was considered really bad.*

Nicole: *Yes, for a boy it's considered a coup, an achievement, to seduce a girl but for a girl to let herself be seduced is a shame. His sexuality meets with approval and hers meets with cheap, slut, things like that.*

I think one of the most destructive things that happened because of this was that you grew up with the idea that it's okay to be a tease. It's okay to use your body, your sexuality, up to a point, to make yourself popular, to get material or status things that you want.

Bruce: *A slut is a broad who'll fuck for a beer. That's my definition of a slut. And she's about fifty years old and it's hangin' out of her pants.*

Stefan: *I think there's no such animal as a slut. The word doesn't mean anything to me.*

Chris: *Any girl who fucks is the same as any guy who fucks.*

Stefan: *Except there are a lot of girls who don't fuck.*

Paul: *Let's see how liberal you really are. How would you define a slut?*

Chris: *Well, it's a word invented by certain males to describe a woman who screws a lot.*

Stefan: *Now, a call girl is a professional girl who really knows how to go about it. She's learned her things and has the same high professional standing as any guy who's gone to school. But the main way to differentiate is that some girls do it for money and some girls don't.*

Bruce: *Why pay money for a piece of ass when you can jerk off and do it to yourself?*

Chris: *I've never paid any woman for any sex I've ever had. Other than in food and drink and travel and whatever else sort of comes with it.*

Stefan: *Which probably costs a hell of a lot more.*

Chris: *Yeah, right.*

Linda: *I remember this girl at school, Anita. She and this friend of hers. They were the school whores. They were both kind of fat and sloppy and were fairly slow in school. They obviously had no self-respect at all. They were like some kind of receptacle. They were totally ostracized by both boys and girls. Everybody knew that they fucked, right, that they did dirty things. I remember once coming into a class in high school and on the desk was "Anita sucks my dick" or something like that.*

Cathy: *How do you know she wasn't proud of herself?*

Amy: *Yeah, because she got recognition some way. Maybe she figured some recognition, no matter what it was for, was better than none at all.*

Linda: *But it was so clear that they had no self-respect.*

Cathy: *I think you'd like to think they had no self-respect but maybe they were very happy. Didn't you ever think you maybe wanted to be one of those girls?*

Linda: *In a sense I would have liked to have more sexual experiences at that age than I did, but at the same time I wouldn't want to be looked at by the world the way she was.*

Paul: *Remember the sort of junior whores we had in high school?*

Chris: *Who could afford one? They were a dollar or something.*

Bruce: *We had one we called "the sandbox".*

Chris: *We had a girl called Susan ———— in our school. Everybody screwed Susan ————.*

Paul: *They were lined up. Everyone knew her name.*

Chris: *She was a nympho. But, like I used to feel sorry for her. I also used to dream about Susan. I always dreamed about who was the first. After that the thrill ended.*

Paul: *Yeah, there was that one first guy that started her goin'. Because she knew next to nothin' when she started. She liked it and she wanted to do everything.*

Bruce: *You got to give the guy a lot of credit. He obviously initiated her cracker.*

Paul: *Her father kicked her out and she had the usual run of VD; then she left town and became a lesbian and then I think she committed suicide.*

What about the sexual revolution? The upheaval in our sexual attitudes seems to have had its psychological casualties, even among the sexually "free" people of the rock world.

They tell you they love you and they tell you this and that just to get you to do what they want. . . . They say words they don't really mean. . . . That's all they want. They build up a whole conversation the whole night and all they want is a fuck. . . . I can get into someone mentally, too. . . .

These chicks really believe that they're gonna meet their Prince Charming and he plays fabulous guitar and he's gonna take them away and marry them.

The Groupies *Earth Records*

The major fuckup on the part of most groupie chicks comes at the point they forget that no matter what goes down they're still women. The same double standard exists in rock society as in the society as a whole. A man may shed every vestige of self-respect and still retain the respect of society because, after all, he is still a man. Not so for a woman.

"Groupies and Other Girls"
A Rolling Stone *Special Report*
John Burks and Jerry Hopkins

The rhetoric of the sexual revolution, if it brought no improvements for women, proved to have great value for men. By convincing women that the usual female games and demands were despicable, unfair, prudish, old-fashioned, puritanical and self-destructive, a new reservoir of available females was created to expand the tight supply of sexual goods available for traditional exploitation, disarming women of even the little protection they had so painfully acquired. Women today dare not make the old demands for fear of having a whole new vocabulary, designed just for this purpose, hurled at them: "fucked up," "ballbreaker," "cockteaser," "a real drag," "a bad trip," etc. To be a "groovy chick" is the idea. . . . But more and more women are sucked into the trap, only to find out too late and bitterly, that the traditional female games had a point.

Shulamith Firestone
The Dialectic of Sex

More traditional sexual attitudes that are damaging to women can be found in a great deal of the "educational" literature that finds its way, with complete social approval, into the hands of young girls.

An example is the following excerpt from a booklet entitled *Your Years of Self-Discovery*, by Kotex Products, Kimberly-Clark of Canada Ltd., which is part of a series widely distributed in Canadian high schools. It perpetuates the idea that women are the objects of sex and not subjective participants in the sexual experience. It teaches that women's sexual feelings are not as strong or as important as those of men. It instructs girls to bear responsibility and blame for the fact that inadvertently they will arouse young boys, and encourages them to be self-conscious of their femaleness. The possibility is never entertained that young boys may be sexually stimulating to young girls.

The Pleasure of Femininity

Straight Talk About the Sex Urge
It is important to acknowledge that you, as a young woman, have a very special responsibility to the young men in your life. Male sexual feelings are aroused, in general, much more quickly and easily than your own. A sweater that merely seems fashionable to you may appear sexually provocative to your date. The necking that you consider as little more than friendly communication may stimulate him to physical passion. Obviously, the best way to cope with this unwanted state of affairs is to avoid setting the stage for it or irresponsibly provoking it. Turn off the heat long, long before your date reaches the boiling point. . . .

Straight Talk About the Sexual Embrace
At the climax of the sexual act the penis ejaculates its semen. Although no similar ejaculation occurs in a woman, this climax is called orgasm in both the male and the female. . . .

Glossary
Clitoris: A small organ at the upper part of the vulva.

Even Sherlock Holmes would have trouble discovering a clue here as to what female orgasm was all about. Feminist writer Anne Koedt is trying to help us to find ourselves, so to speak.

Frigidity has generally been defined by men as the failure of women to have vaginal orgasms. Actually the vagina is not a highly sensitive area and is not constructed to achieve orgasm. . . . There is only one area for sexual arousal; that area is the clitoris. All orgasms are extensions of sensation from this area. Since the clitoris is not necessarily stimulated sufficiently in the conventional sexual positions, we are left "frigid". . . .

Men have orgasms essentially by friction with the vagina, not the clitoral area. . . . Women have thus been defined sexually in terms of what pleases men; our own biology has not been properly analyzed. Instead we are fed the myth of the liberated woman and her vaginal orgasm—an orgasm which in fact does not exist. . . .

Perhaps one of the most infuriating and damaging results of this whole charade has been that women who were perfectly healthy sexually were taught that they were not. So in addition to being sexually deprived, these women were told to blame themselves when they deserved no blame. Looking for a cure to a problem that has none can lead a woman on an endless path of self-hatred and insecurity.

Anne Koedt
The Myth of the Vaginal Orgasm

Insofar as it serves to give women the confidence to assert their sexual needs and tune in to their own bodies, Anne Koedt's paper is of value. But she goes on to use the fact that women can achieve orgasm without male penetration as an intellectual rationale for lesbianism. At one point, she rather gleefully gloats over a fantasy of castration.

Lesbian sexuality could make an excellent case, based upon anatomical data, for the extinction of the male organ. Albert Ellis says something to the effect that a man without a penis can make a woman an excellent lover.

Also strongly disputed is her cocksure claim that there is no such thing as "vaginal orgasm"; that any woman who says she has experienced one is either ignorant of her own body or "lying to 'get the job' ". Germaine Greer, author of *The Female Eunuch*, disagrees:

The substitution of the clitoral spasm for genuine gratification may turn out to be a disaster for sexuality. . . . It is nonsense to say that a woman feels nothing when a man is moving his penis in her vagina: the orgasm is qualitatively different when the vagina can undulate around the penis instead of a vacancy.

Amy: *It's interesting this whole thing about the clitoris being ignored lots of times. A man doesn't care that that's what gives you pleasure.*

Gloria: *But lots of times a man doesn't even know, and there's no way that you can tell him.*

Amy: *My ex-husband and I lived together for six months before we got married and we had plenty of time to talk about it. I was very frank about it. We discussed what gave each other pleasure, but he didn't seem to think about it. I guess he just got carried away with the whole thing. It made me very angry, very hostile, very upset. The man I live with now is much more considerate.*

Linda: *There used to be times for me when it was difficult to communicate what I wanted because I didn't want to hurt his ego or blow it for him. But you can work these things out.*

Amy: *It's not necessarily trying to spare his feelings all the time. You don't want to make something mechanical out of something natural.*

Gloria: *Is sex such a natural thing? My level of response now is something I've learned. I've learned to respond. Perhaps the emphasis shouldn't be on the natural as much as it is.*

Nicole: *One of the first things about sex that I remember being told was when my grandmother explained the Bible story of creation to me. She said that because Adam ate of the fruit of the tree, sex came into the world as punishment for Eve—childbirth and sex.*

Linda: *Yes, when you're a kid, even while you're reading* True Story *and getting hot, at the same time you always remember it's supposed to hurt the first time. That was always the big fear my girlfriends and I would talk about. Sex and childbirth are always supposed to hurt. And it sure did the first few times. And there was blood the first two.*

Ellen: *I remember my first time. I wasn't impressed at all.*

Chris: *My first time was by accident. I was playing around with this girl's cunt and it happened to go up the right bloody hole. We really didn't know what the hell we were doing. Like I was playing around with her for a couple of months before I figured out how to break in. It was completely by accident and I suddenly found myself in this nice, luscious spot. For about thirty seconds or so I couldn't figure out what the hell I had done. Then I started coming so I pulled myself out because I realized I might be doing something. So I came outside and that was really disappointing, but I was worried about getting her pregnant. As a matter of fact, that's been my major worry whenever I've screwed any broad—knocking them up.*

Stefan: *My first time was with a girl after a party at my house. We got undressed and we were petting and then came the most difficult part—getting it in. But then I just kind of got it in and I was in there for about thirty seconds and I was afraid to move because I was going to come inside her. So finally, I pulled out and came right away. But the first time I ever had a really good lay was with a French-Canadian girl who was working at my uncle's place. She had the greatest boobs and the greatest black bra you've ever seen.*

Chris: *I think the first four times I tried screwing different girls they still had their panties on. I discovered this technique where you pull the bottom of the panty down and shove the damn thing in before they realize what's happening. But man, it was a bloody fight every time.*

Linda: *It's something that develops. Like, when you're in your teens, before you actually have sex, when you're making out or masturbating you have purely clitoral orgasms and they can be very strong. But then I found the first time I ever fucked, aside from the fact that it was painful, it was a totally foreign sensation. Because between petting and intercourse is a kind of bridge that you have to cross. But once you really accept him in you, then there really is a difference in the kind of orgasmic experience that you have.*

Nicole: *One assumption is that the orgasm is the only sexual response possible. That you have to have an orgasm every time. That it can't be just sort of good. There may be difficulties in having an orgasm every time, but even when you don't reach it, it's not a total loss. It's still a communication with the other person.*

Cathy: *Well, before, women never felt they had any right to an orgasm, and now they want it right or wrong.*

Linda: *What do you mean right or wrong?*

Cathy: *Well, I'm not convinced that women should have an orgasm every time they make love. I think a lot of women feel that if they're going to make love then they bloody well should have an orgasm. I would like to, too. But I think you have to accept that you won't always.*

Linda: *But why should anyone want to accept that?*

Cathy: *I've learned to accept it.*

Gloria: *Well, I accept it too because I often don't have an orgasm when I make love.*

Cathy: *I think it's a mistake to be really intolerant about it. If I felt I had a right to an orgasm every time I made love then I would become upset and hostile towards the person I was making love to and I'd sort of be a mess, wouldn't I?*

Chris: *I'm not worried about impotence. I haven't had too many bad experiences.*

Bruce: *Have you ever been impotent?*

Chris: *No.*

Paul: *No, no, no problems either.*

Stefan: *It happens to me when I drink champagne. I once got some champagne and was going to play the great lover and then when it came time to perform there was nothing.*

Paul: *Well, most guys are too fast. They don't know how to control.*

Chris: *How do you guys keep from coming too soon?*

Bruce: *I'll tell you how. I do it by thinking about bridge hands. I'm serious. Bridge hands.*

Paul: *That's right. You put your mind off. Then it disappears but you can get it right up again to a peak and let it down. You can go on like that for hours.*

Bruce: *Another way to do it is to have the female on top of you doing all her thing. She could be going a mile a minute. Then I have to think hard to come with her.*

Every now and then the Sensuous Woman finds it necessary to pull out of her bag of pleasure one of her top skills—The Sarah Bernhardt.

She acts.

No woman would refuse to make love to a man she cares for just because she "doesn't really feel like it." You focus like mad on all the fantasies that stir your sexual juices, concentrate on making your body respond to the highest point possible and, if you really can't get to orgasm, to avoid disappointing him and spoiling his plateau of excitement and sexiness, you fake that orgasm.

To become a fabulous fake, study again every contortion, muscle spasm and body response that lead to and make up the orgasm and rehearse the process privately until you can duplicate it.

But . . . you must never, never, reveal to him that you have acted sometimes in bed.

You will betray a trust shared by every other female in the world if you do.

> *The Sensuous Woman*
> by J

Amy: *Has anyone ever pretended to have an orgasm? I know I have . . . because I feel inadequate as a lover. So I pretend and although I enjoy it sometimes, I pretend the greater part of the time that I'm in ecstasy when I'm not really.*

Ellen: *The times that I have pretended I've pretended for that reason. Not so much caring for the man's feelings but for myself. I don't want him to think that there's something wrong with me.*

Linda: *I had pretended with a man and told him long after I had stopped pretending. But he was very hurt to find this out. And angry. And I don't blame him for being angry because it's just really depressing to think about dishonesty between people at the time when they're the closest. . . .*

Ellen: *Well now, with this whole sexual revolution thing —the day suddenly appeared when you had to be satisfied. Here you are being repressed all your life and now the gates are open girls, you can admit that you enjoy it. And instead we're saying, hell, I haven't enjoyed it at all. And so you had to pretend to cover that.*

Nicole: *I don't think I had an orgasm for about three years after I lost my virginity. And I think I had it because I was high. And, you know, you really feel inadequate if you don't have it.*

Gloria: *Yes, you know, for a long time I was really conscious, you know, that I had to have an orgasm. And it didn't come. And you know, you're supposed to have it. Like you read in books.*

Cathy: *I'd be interested to know what everyone here thinks of passion. I think having orgasms is feeling passion and. . . .*

Linda: *It's different from feeling passion. Passion is something kind of generalized, where an orgasm is something very specific that lasts a certain amount of time.*

Cathy: *It ends itself. It's complete. Is that what you mean?*

Linda: *It's complete. It's got a beginning and an end. And it kind of builds up and explodes and spreads . . . it's . . . it's fucking hard to describe.*

Cathy: *But what I'm wondering is if you can have an orgasm without feeling passion.*

Linda: *To me, passion is in your mind when things are at the fantasy stage, but horny is horny and it's right between your legs.*

Bruce: *There's two things that give me pleasure in sex. One is the game in gettin' there and the other is to drive a broad out of her mind. That is as much, if not more, pleasure than doing it yourself.*

Paul: *The thing is, get her there, if that is possible, and keep here there as long as you can. Once you do that you know you can go any old time you want and she's gonna be happy when she's finished.*

Bruce: *If you play the game right you can get her to go two or three times. And you hit any one of them in there and you're fine.*

Chris: *I wonder if women really enjoy sex. This is something I've never really figured out. I know they go into all these fantastic ecstasies and everything, but. . . .*

Gloria: *I'd like to talk about frigidity because . . . I think I'd qualify as a frigid person.*

Amy: *So would I.*

Gloria: *I'd like to talk about it but I don't really know what to say.*

Amy: *What makes you think you're frigid?*

Gloria: *Well, there are times when I can be very sexually aroused but by the time it's at its height I can feel the muscles around my vagina tightening. It can be very painful and I really have to concentrate on relaxing to work that out.*

Amy: *What I find often happens a lot is that I'll be very interested. I'll even initiate the action, you know. Go up to him, and kiss him, and things. And then when we both get aroused and it comes right down to the actual thing, then all of a sudden I don't want to. And it's the most horrible feeling in the world for me and terrible for him. And he's always really kind about it and that's what makes me feel like I'm frigid. Because when it comes right down to it, then all of a sudden my whole body's just turned off and I'm not interested. And then I don't know what to do anymore. Does that happen to anyone else?*

(A few people say yes.)

Amy: *Did you ever consider the penis your enemy?*

Gloria: *What do you mean?*

Ellen: *Yeah, Explain that.*

Amy: *Well, the first time I ever verbalized it was the other day. I was talking to Pete, the guy I'm living with now, and I said: "You know, I consider your penis my enemy." I feel like it's attacking me . . . I guess . . . I really feel like it's my enemy. I don't like him to go around the house without underpants on. I don't like him to come to bed naked. I like him to have a night shirt on, or underpants. Because I don't like it to touch me when I'm not expecting it. Maybe I'm abnormal.*

Gloria: *No, I don't think so. It's probably that no one ever talks about it.*

Ellen: *No, I know what you mean. Um, the most problematical area for me—I'm kind of embarrassed to mention it, but I will—I don't like to look at a man's balls or his penis. I like what they do but I don't like to look at them. And I've always thought there must be something wrong with me. That was the only thing I was really inhibited about. When it came to doing what he asked me because it would please him, I would do it, but I never looked at it. I always felt there was something ugly about a man's genitals.*

Chris: *Sometimes you can look at a woman's cunt and say what a fucking ugly mess.*

Stefan: *It feels slimy.*

Bruce: *I'm very leery of screwing something unless I know it's hygienically clean. There's nothing worse than a smelly cunt. If it's been freshly washed you know you're gettin' the goods.*

A delicate problem... solved gently. **Femfresh.**

Ignoring vaginal odour won't make it go away. New Femfresh will. It's one of Europe's leading vaginal deodorants. Femfresh is dry. Gentle. And effective. It stops bacteria growth on the outer skin—where odours start. Use Femfresh every day to feel completely clean. Femfresh. In two tender fragrances. Fougère. And Fleur. As feminine as you are.

Should one suppose that men naturally secrete their own "Femfresh"?

Amy: *I was with a man once and it was the first time for him. And you know what he said. He said it's like putting your penis in a sticky hole.*

Ellen: *Someone told me about a girl of about twenty-two or twenty-three. She married this law student and they went to Acapulco for their honeymoon. And afterward she said she had been totally appalled by sex. And she didn't know what she was going to do. She was just . . . sickened by it. Physically sick. They'd never had any kind of sexual intercourse before the night of their wedding and that night when her husband got undressed she looked at his genitals and got really sick. Because that was the first time she had ever looked at a man's penis. And she went into the bathroom and vomited.*

Women are the only "love" objects in our society. So much so that women regard themselves as erotic. Women can be fulfilled sexually only by vicarious identification with the man who enjoys them.

Shulamith Firestone
The Dialectic of Sex

Here is another variation on the theme of man as the subject of experience and woman as the object. Perhaps you've guiltily perused your man's *Playboy* magazines. Well, it doesn't mean you're queer. If you find pictures of nude women sexy it's because you see yourself as her. You imagine a man looking at her (you) and becoming excited, and this in turn excites you.

It's interesting to note that even magazines catering to a female audience are full of pictures of women in sexually provocative poses. We've heard men say that *Cosmopolitan* covers rival *Playboy*. *Vogue* magazine quite often features erotic female nudes.

What all of this means is that we respond to men indirectly and not directly. In a sexual situation it might mean that you are excited by his being excited by you. You are not directly responding to him. It might also make you self-conscious—how closely does your body compare to those idealized magazine pictures?

Discover the Source of Body Beauty

Your body. A complexion stretching down to your toes. With a language
all its own. Now Frances Denney introduces seven new Sources of Beauty
to silken and tone your skin all over. To cleanse, enrich, revitalize it.
Blue, light, cooling sources for morning use . . . golden rich ones
for evening lavishment. A complete body care collection created by

Frances Denney

Wake-up Bath Crystals □ Exhilarating Body Pick-up □ Moisture Body Veil □ Bathing Spa □ Ultra Smoothing Oil Bath □ Lavish Body Finish □ Bust and Body Firmer

Another unhealthy element in this process is narcissism—perhaps even a kind of masturbatory narcissism. In magazine ads women admire themselves, touch themselves, or stare out blankly in a stupor of self-adoration. And there is something about the stupidity and vulnerability of some of these poses that invites humiliation. It's interesting to note, too, that an important aspect of a great deal of pornography is its degradation of the female.

news from 'Moon Drops'

Chris: Seeing *fucking really turns me on. The first great picture I ever saw was in grade eight. This guy brought in his brother's pictures of a girl getting fucked. A guy was sitting there and he had his balls between her tits and she was eating him out. She was lying on her back. It was really great.*

Stefan: *Stag movies. I've seen one in which there was this girl and a dog.*

Bruce: *I've seen a girl and a donkey for real in Tijuana. But there was one stag movie that was the rottenest stag movie I've ever seen. It was called the "Golden Jet". There was a broad lying in a bathtub and there were three guys standing around the bathtub and they were pissing on her.*

Stefan: *I saw one in which this broad sits on a chair and she's all tied up to this chair, you see, and they make her pee into a glass and then they make her drink the glass.*

Chris: *I don't get turned on by stag movies anymore.*

Paul: *You'd be sick if you were.*

Bruce: *There's this great topless club in California. The broads are generally relatively dumb but good lookin' and they do this runway bit and you sit under the runway so you got snatch about five inches from your nose. They go snakeshit if you're Canadian. There were six of them when I was there and I could have had a piece there from any one of three. One even gave me a discount rate. She charges $75 regularly. She was a good-lookin' broad, really good-lookin', the only one I've seen with an educated snatch. It was just like a puppet. No kiddin'. It was an evening of fun for $15.*

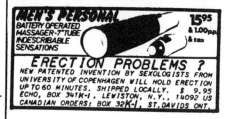

Nicole: *Did you ever get the feeling when you're talking to some men that they're not listening to you at all? They couldn't care less. They're just looking at you, just sizing up the visual.*

Ellen: *Well, when I feel like a man is taking me in visually, I like it. Because if he wasn't appreciating what I looked like, I'd be wondering what was wrong with me.*

Linda: *Well, it's so hard to walk down the street in front of a group of men and not feel self-conscious. You can pretend you're not, but they know you know they're watching. Sometimes maybe you feel like smiling, but other times you say, damn it, what right do they have to invade my privacy this way.*

Amy: *This morning I ran for the bus and they were digging up the trolley tracks and there were all these guys working on them. And they're all going, "Ahhh, honey, sweetie." Well, I got on that bus and I was livid. I hate it because they don't know me and I'm nothing but a female body to them and it infuriates me.*

Linda: *Sometimes you're not even a whole body to them. You're legs, or tits, or ass. It's like being chopped up in sections.*

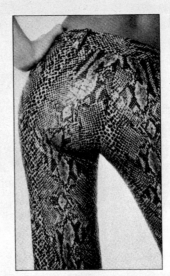
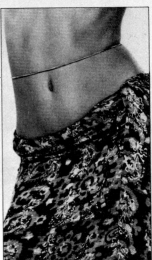

Nicole: *There's something I've been wanting to talk about that's been a problem to me personally. I think I'm probably the only one here who's just had a single sexual partner who is her husband. And I feel that it was probably because of certain social pressures that I married the first man that I slept with. And so I've always felt sort of cheated and inexperienced and like I don't really know where it's at. And I know damn well that some day I'm going to be unfaithful to him. And I don't like the idea that that's what I have to be. And I'm sure that he would kill me or do something extremely violent. But all the same, I feel I'm getting older—I'm twenty-four, and that's not really old—but I'm sort of getting older all the time and eventually I'll be unattractive to men and I won't have done all those things you can do only if you're young and attractive.*

Ellen: *Well, I've got something I've kind of wanted to say, too. Like, my husband isn't the first man I've slept with but I didn't sleep with many. Like those experiences you had, Linda, like I really envy you for that.*

Linda: *But in a way it was really rough. You know, I hopped in and out of an awful lot of beds before I was* married and if physical satisfaction is the criterion then a lot of them were okay. But like, once I slept with this guy I didn't care for at all. I had no interest in him except that at that particular time I felt horny and he was around. But after, I felt used. Because *he saw it that way and because no matter what the reality of it was in my head, it's always the guy's conquest. He could brag that he made me.*

Bruce: *Ahhh, here is the problem. A man can have sex without attachments. Most women cannot enjoy sex unless they have some sort of an attachment. They equate sex and love. I don't give a shit for that. But they screw because she has a feeling for the guy or for security. Of course, there are some who can just screw, but they're all nymphos or they want to do it for hire.*

Amy: *When I was asked to come here to talk about sex I phoned my best friend to tell her about it. And we were talking and I said to her, "Now, this is in the strictest confidence. I have to say that I really don't enjoy it that much, so I guess I'm sort of abnormal." And she said: "Well, I can only remember about three times in my life that I enjoyed it. Most of the time I really enjoy the cuddling and being loved before and after, so I just sort of fake it to get it over with so I can be cuddled again." And I said that I really felt the same way and that lots of times I pretend. And I mean, here we are best friends and we'd never talked about it before. She thought I was having this great time and I thought she was.*

But I really do think some of the problems I've expressed are abnormal. I really think they are.

Everyone: *No, no. I don't think so. You shouldn't feel that way.*

Amy: *My whole life I've really resented the male role of trying to get something from my body before trying to appreciate me as a person. Now, I started very young and had a very active sexual life very early, and I found that boys or men would play games, would do anything, just to get what they wanted. I remember in college there was this fellow I went out with a whole year and I would never allow anything to happen because I knew the minute I did the game would be over. And one night he got me drunk especially for that, and we did it. And he gloated. He told everyone at school. And really good men friends of mine would come up and say: "Oh, Amy. I hear your're really a hot number. Why didn't you let me in on some of the action." Stuff like that has made me so bitter that I think it has a lot to do with my freezing up at the last minute. I really just thought of that and so this discussion has been really good for me because of that. Because I've been sitting here trying to analyze why all these things happened. Even with the guy I'm living with now, who I really feel loves me and isn't taking advantage of me. When it comes down to the crux, at the last minute, I think he's just being nice to me because he wants something. I think that's really messed me up a whole lot.*

In case this chapter has left any doubt that female sexual problems are induced by societal attitudes towards women, let us close with this possible explanation of why female sexuality has been suppressed so long and so much.

No doubt the most far-reaching hypothesis extrapolated from biological data is the existence of the universal and physically normal condition of women's inability ever to reach complete sexual satiation in the presence of the most intense, repetitive orgasmic experience, no matter how produced. Theoretically, a woman could go on having orgasms indefinitely if physical exhaustion did not intervene. . . .

It is conceivable that the forceful suppression of women's inordinate sexual demands was a prerequisite to the dawn of every modern civilization and almost every living culture. Primitive woman's sexual drive was too strong, too susceptible to the fluctuating extremes of an impelling, aggressive erotism to withstand the disciplined requirements of a settled family life. . . .

Not until these drives were gradually brought under control by rigidly enforced social codes could family life become the stabilizing and creative crucible from which modern civilized man could emerge. . . .

The strength of the drive determines the force required to suppress it.

Mary Jane Sherfey, M.D.
A Theory on Female Sexuality

Marriage

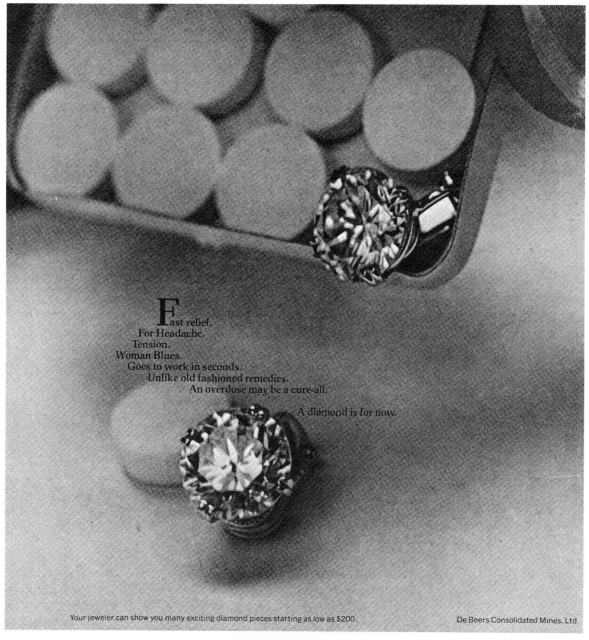

ast relief.
For Headache.
Tension.
Woman Blues.
Goes to work in seconds.
Unlike old fashioned remedies.
An overdose may be a cure-all.

A diamond is for now.

Your jeweler can show you many exciting diamond pieces starting as low as $200.   De Beers Consolidated Mines, Ltd.

Stay home little girl, stay home
Don't roam, little girl, don't roam
The girl who stays home is a fool they may
　　say
But she's just the kind they marry some
　　day....

(Popular song from the twenties)

After going steady comes marriage, if life is to progress in an orderly fashion, and it generally does.

On Becoming a Woman
Mary M. Williams and Irene Kane

If independence is a necessary concomitant of freedom, women must not marry.

Germaine Greer
The Female Eunuch

Is marriage the ideal state for woman or is it merely "the denial of life", as Germaine Greer suggests? Both of these concepts are extreme, but they represent the conflict faced by the married woman: on the one hand marriage can be terribly confining, yet on the other hand alternative ways of living as a woman remain ill-defined.

Few if any women marry for love alone. Part of their motivation is the search for a socially accepted role and the rewards it brings. Certainly marriage can provide pleasures and joys; when two self-confident individuals are sharing equally, giving and taking, then marriage is a creative and healthy experience. But as a bribe for emotional and material security, marriage can be destructive to the woman; when she depends utterly on her husband for survival, rides on his abilities, seeks her identity through him alone, the relationship can only damage her in the long run by making her forever vulnerable.

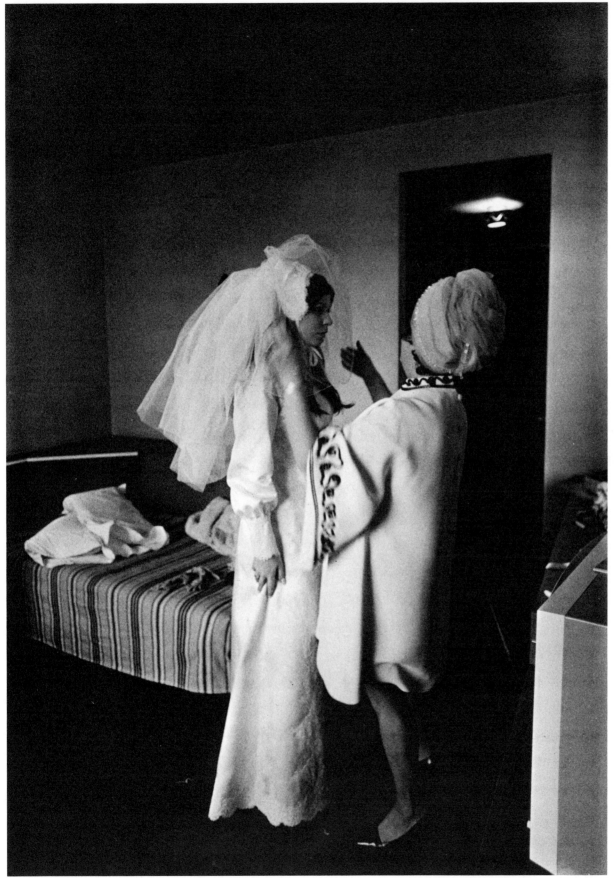

Laura Jones

The wedding ceremony itself symbolizes this state of being. As Germaine Greer writes in *The Female Eunuch*, "The wedding is the chief ceremony of the middle-class mythology, and it functions as the official entree of the spouses to their middle-class status." The ceremony, with its attendant cult of bridal gowns, showers, silverware patterns, photographers, honeymoons and home decorating, emphasizes the myth of female purity and innocence, foreshadowing a strict masculine-feminine role-definition in which the wife becomes a domestic creature, a dependent.

As working women will testify, this role-division manifests itself strongly even if the wife holds a job. The male is still considered the prime supporter, the female the prime tension manager, responsible for smoothing over emotional crises and smoothing the marriage's nervous twitches. She generally retains the domestic burdens of cooking and cleaning, in addition to her job in the outside world. And while her husband finds that his married state is no barrier to forming interesting relationships with women, the wife is cut off from friendships with other men—she is a marked woman, rendered ineligible for a wide range of experiences.

Today, as women begin to seek broader social involvements, the restrictive view of marriage must inevitably wither away.

In the following pages two different kinds of women describe their expectations of marriage, their actual experiences of it, and their reasons for abandoning it. The first, Anne, a well-educated, career-trained, middle-class woman, was married for twenty-two years before she became divorced at the age of forty-one. She was initially shocked by the idea of separation, of discovering that the eternal guarantee of love, protection and security no longer exists. She was surprised to find that her present state of single-ness and independence is enjoyable.

In the second part of the chapter we hear from Christine, whose experience as a young conventional housewife, living at home with a child, runs contrary to the widespread expectations of house-and-happiness. Her first stab at independence from her parents' home was the opportunity to marry. She took it, but experienced a new kind of dependency, a sense of personal inadequacy due to lack of a skill that might have given her a life she could call her own. "I was nothing," she says. "My husband was my support." As a housewife her choice was to please her man or forfeit the security he represented. Not until she acquired a specific skill did Christine attain any feelings of confidence and self-esteem. As soon as she became qualified for a profession, she was no longer wholly dependent on her husband for survival and was able to think clearly about her own identity. She is now divorced, working, supporting her child and involved in a relationship with another man. But her ideas about marriage and woman's role have changed.

Both of these women's stories are edited versions of interview transcripts.

In this chapter we have concentrated on women who are no longer married. By so doing we don't intend to imply that marrage is undesirable; we wish merely to discuss the factors that often make it so, to illustrate the conditions that prevent women from dealing wisely with marriage. Many of the feelings and unfulfilled expectations discussed by these two women are similar. Although their experiences may differ in degree and in result with others', they do serve to point out the great gap that exists between the promise of marriage and its reality. So often we hear of successful marriages and contented housewives, or how unsatisfactory marriages have been improved or "saved". But too rarely do we have the opportunity to explore the reasons that make some relationships impossible to resolve. And too rarely do we read of how women have managed happily with divorce, after being accustomed previously to a protected environment, or of women who have taken the gamble—choosing not to accept the sometime myth that a bad marriage is better than none at all.

© 1970 Jules Feiffer

Anne: *I was a most naive nineteen-year-old girl when I got married twenty-two years ago. It was simply a question of falling in love with someone. At that time I felt I could conquer the world. There was nothing that I couldn't do. There was no possibility that my marriage wouldn't be a success once I married.*

My husband was a lowly student when I married him. I felt there was a promise of status from him. And while we were married, that became a fact of life.

My husband wanted the kind of woman who would stand for hours cooking lasagna and look like a glamour girl at the same time, and also, if possible, be a career woman. There were certain expectations or hopes on his part that I would do all of these things including many other things outside the house. In some respects I think he regarded me as a good showpiece.

My husband was very successful in business. I felt pride for him, and became dependent on his success. He had contacts with all kinds of interesting people. And because he did, I did too. Everywhere he went, I went. He was the kind of guy who came home, grabbed my hand and said, "Look, we're going out." This is what I missed most after the divorce. The sudden loss of all these friends.

I found it difficult to maintain the same friendships after the divorce. The main reason I think was that I was suddenly single and they were married and our lives no longer meshed. You find yourself no longer appropriate for many kinds of activities because you are just a woman alone. I also had a feeling that some of the women were scared of me.

Not only did I feel defined by my husband's success, but I was defined by my role as a mother. I was defined too by many things which I myself did during the marriage. Even though I did not work, I was always running off to take a university course. I did not let my own life go completely, although certainly it was kept to a minimum compared to what it would have been if I hadn't had children.

One of the problems I had to solve after the divorce was finding myself again. I had lived quite a physically active life; always on the go. One year I finished my postgraduate studies, was president of my local riding association and cared for four children. I was running around like mad all the while wondering if that was really me. I think I wanted to do all those activities, but they were compressed into such a small time span that I didn't have any time left over to think about me. That was not my pace. That was his. I had extended his manner of living to become my own.

Our divorce was caused by another woman for whom my husband left me. But that was really just the final factor. There were countless reasons—his approaching middle age, fear of impotence, the feeling that his life was passing by. These were not all verbalized but understood. We married very young and consequently my husband had had very little experience with women. He felt he had missed his adolescence by marrying— that he had never gone through the wild period that a lot of boys do. He had a deprived feeling. He was left with a deprived feeling about the marriage and I wasn't; even though the fact was that I had given up a great deal for my marriage. I was trained for a profession which I did not get to work in until after the divorce; instead, I did useless volunteer work in order to try to put meaning into my life. Most of the time I had a pre-schooler around, and, being a very conscientious mother, I used to hang around the house most of the time. That was what probably contributed to what finally happened to our relationship. It was interesting that he married a woman who was working; he was quite verbal about the fact that she had proved herself out in the world as a professional person. But humorously enough, now she's home with the baby and I'm out working.

I feel better about myself now than I have at any time since I've been an adult. The divorce came as a shock to me—I had a year-old baby at the time and three other children—and I had always taken for granted, especially when I married, that this would be forever. I never questioned that we would live happily together for the rest of our lives. Now I know that such security thinking is illogical and unreal.

I miss the fact now that I don't have an extremely close relationship with a man. I have many boyfriends but not one very close relationship. I'm not mentioning the word marriage here because that isn't necessarily what it would have to be. I am not sure now about the investment in marriage. I had always felt as a little girl that I would be married and that it would be permanent, forever, and that the investment I would make would be worth it. There was no question in my mind. But now I wonder. I'm not sure I wouldn't prefer a limited kind of investment, one that would be less than a full legal marriage.

The longer I am divorced, the less eager I am to get married. I started out from the break-up with the feeling that if I were not married within two or three years I'd be ready to jump off a bridge. That is how I projected into the future. Yet the exact reverse has happened.

My children are partly responsible. They are part of my community. But the major reason is that my own psychological well-being has been rising over the past few years while other aspects of my life have fallen into place. The divorce made possible a reorganization within my own personality. All this change in me would not have occurred without such a drastic break with the past. I think it's almost impossible in an ongoing situation to be objective enough to change your life radically, or your situation. Only drastic measures like analysis or separation seem to enforce real changes.

At the time of the divorce, I felt there would be only one condition under which I would welcome this breaking up—if I could just meet my next ideal man and marry him. But that hasn't worked out, and in a sense I'm very happy that it hasn't. At one time I never would have imagined myself saying this. But now I can see myself, I'm really a better person. I look back on my marriage and see periods of depression; whereas now I wake up in the mornings and jump happily out of bed.

In my former relationship I was the one who gave more. I feel now that in any future close relationship with a man both of us would have to be willing to over-extend ourselves. I didn't go into marriage thinking that way. I went in feeling I could give and give. I think it was very unrealistic.

The reaction of my family and friends to my present state of happiness in being single is that, if I don't re-marry someday, I'll be all alone. People who say things like that, I feel, are projecting. Some of them are envious and cannot stand the thought that I can get along living alone and enjoy it. I think it is almost incomprehensible to some of them.

52★   TORONTO DAILY STAR, Tues., July 20, 1971

Ann Landers

Ten secrets of a happy marriage

Dear Ann Landers: After a quarter of a century of marriage I have finally learned the secret of a happy marriage. I have listed ten rules, which I guarantee will work for all couples. Of course these rules are for women. In our society there are no rules for men.

1. If he says, "I won't be home for dinner tonight, don't wait up for me," don't ask where he is going. Such a question gives the impression you do not trust him.

2. If he comes in very late, don't ask where he has been. Such a question gives the impression you are insecure.

3. Keep his clothes in perfect condition.

4. Keep his stomach full.

5. Keep his car clean.

6. Keep the kids quiet and away from him when he comes home at night. Questions can drive a father crazy—especially if he doesn't know the answers.

7. Give him plenty of sex no matter how tired you are or what kind of a day you've had.

8. Don't ask him for money.

9. Starve yourself if you must, but stay a size 10 forever. Never mention the fact that he has gained 30 pounds and the seams in his pants are splitting.

10. Don't tell him your troubles. A woman who stays home all day shouldn't have any.—MARRIAGE MAVIN IN PHILADELPHIA.

Dear Mavin: Thanks for letting us know what it takes to keep a marriage together in the City of Brotherly Love. Many a truth is spoken in jest.

Christine: *I was seventeen when I married and he was twenty-five. I was in a shaky situation at the time. I thought, it can't be too bad to marry him. I knew he was in love with me. And I figured that he wouldn't leave me, so I married him. I would be living on my own, at last, wouldn't have to worry about staying at home, or supporting myself.*

I felt I loved him at the time. Now I think I was in love with the idea of marriage, not with Tom himself.

I too was afraid of never getting married, even at seventeen. I was extremely boy-conscious, but no one seemed to show any interest in me in high school. I was a wallflower. I really felt insecure. Marriage, I felt, was something I had to do before I got over twenty. I was worried about this lack of attention. Everyone else seemed to be getting attention, everyone else seemed happy in relationships. I could not get anyone.

At that time I was sure marriage to Tom was what I wanted. It was both romantic and practical. I wouldn't have to worry about anything after that. I had stars in my eyes when I got married.

Afterwards we started having little conflicts. We had different preferences. I had definite ideas about what I wanted for furniture, for example, but was always afraid to tell him "This is what I want." I felt he was the boss, that maybe I owed him a lot for doing what he did in marrying me, for even being in love with me. I thought I owed him for it.

He made me feel that I should be thankful to him for my new-found affluence. My family never had any savings and he had saved an awful lot of money; he seemed really reliable. Living with my family I had never had new clothes; my mother always got them from a rummage sale, or someone else. I never went out to buy things. And suddenly, here I was able to buy things myself. And yet I never felt they belonged to me. I married him with nothing of my own, and so felt even toward the end that his property and money were not really mine.

I worked for a little while after we were married. I gave him each pay cheque, felt I didn't have the right to do otherwise. I owed it to him. He was my husband. Even if I made some money I felt it was his because we were married. But he never gave me any of his money, except cash for shopping and necessary household items. Everything belonged to him. The bank account was in his name. Many times I had no money in my pocket, yet I would still refuse to ask him for money. I was afraid.

I didn't feel equal to him. I always felt I should be good to him because that is what a wife is supposed to do. I always kept my misgivings to myself. But I was getting very uptight. One day, while I was alone, I felt I couldn't work anymore—I got up in the morning, cleaned the place, and got to feeling "I want to do something" but I didn't know what. I didn't want to sit down, go for a walk, go to sleep, stay awake; I would start something but couldn't finish it. It went on that way all day. I tried to watch television but couldn't. I went out on the balcony. Came back inside. I was just walking, racing around the place. When he came home my neck started to feel very stiff. We went out on the balcony. I was talking to him and then started to panic. All of a sudden I grabbed on to him. I felt something inside my head pulling back my neck and eyes. The muscle was being contracted and my eyes were being held up there. I couldn't bring them down. At the hospital I was given medication to force relaxation.

I told my doctor about the incident and other tension headaches I would have intermittently. He told me it was nerves. I had never realized I was really nervous. I think I did worry about this marriage situation of inequality and lack of togetherness, without being aware of it.

I felt less than he was. He was the man, he was working. I would have preferred to be in his position. It seemed I had to look up to him. I admired him and felt like I should always be doing things for him— being whatever he wanted me to be. My responsibility as wife was to show him how much I cared for him— how much I owed him. When he came home at three o'clock in the morning from work I used to be up out of bed making him sandwiches and coffee. I'd do it without any questions.

At this particular time I was not working. I had made various excuses, so he never made me go back to work. Later I did work for a while in a bank but disliked it and quit. The position was menial, I was just another cog in the wheel. So in that case I preferred to be at home. I know I had more talent than what I put into the bank job . . . except I couldn't get the kind of job I wanted since I was still very young (eighteen) and inexperienced.

At least I kept him happy. And he thought I was a good wife. All the guys he brought home commented, "More people should have a wife like that" because I looked after them really well.

One thing I had liked about working was my association with the world. Actually going out to work, I felt like I was part of people, even just going on the subway. Everyone else was doing it too and I was among them, instead of sitting by myself at home.

In the apartment I felt isolated from everything. There were many things happening out in the world, yet I didn't know, I wasn't aware of their activity. I'd turn on the radio to find out what was really going on in the world, to get a feeling of belonging to it. I was not doing anything, contributing my influence to the good or the

*bad of events. I was just being there, listening to what
everyone else was doing, not doing anything myself.
The radio was the only contact I had with the real world.
 I thought I had more of a purpose when I was having
my child. I went to childbirth classes and wanted Tom
to go with me. But he refused, even though I hoped
he would come to understand the activity of birth. At*

these classes I saw other women, other housewives like myself. And I was shocked at how ignorant some of them were. They were happy and content to stay in their homes, they were frowsy, stupid and frumpy. When I saw them I hoped I would never get to be like that. I didn't want to grow into that kind of a woman— a housewife. No wonder people look down on women

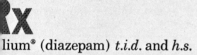

Rx

lium® (diazepam) *t.i.d.* and *h.s.*

A. (Fine Arts)...PTA (President-elect)...representations of a life ently centered around home and children, with too little time to sue a vocation for which she has spent many years in training...a ation that may bespeak continuous frustration and stress: a perfect nework for her to translate the functional symptoms of psychic ion into major problems. For this kind of patient—with no onstrable pathology yet with repeated complaints—consider the inctive properties of Valium® (diazepam). Valium possesses a ounced calming action that usually relieves psychic tension nptly, helping to attenuate the related somatic signs and symptoms. um is generally well tolerated. On proper maintenance age, Valium seldom dulls the senses or interferes with functioning.

en an *h.s.* dose is added to the *t.i.d.* schedule, Valium helps iter sleeplessness due to psychic tension.

re prescribing, please consult complete product information, a summary of a follows:
·ations: Tension and anxiety states; somatic complaints which are concomi- of emotional factors; psychoneurotic states manifested by tension, anxiety, ehension, fatigue, depressive symptoms or agitation; acute agitation, tremor, um tremens and hallucinosis due to acute alcohol withdrawal; adjunctively in tal muscle spasm due to reflex spasm to local pathology, spasticity caused by r motor neuron disorders, athetosis, stiff-man syndrome, convulsive disorders for sole therapy).
raindicated: Known hypersensitivity to the drug. Children under 6 months of Acute narrow angle glaucoma.
nings: Not of value in psychotic patients. Caution against hazardous occupa- requiring complete mental alertness. When used adjunctively in convulsive ders, possibility of increase in frequency and/or severity of grand mal seizures require increased dosage of standard anticonvulsant medication; abrupt with- al may be associated with temporary increase in frequency and/or severity of res. Advise against simultaneous ingestion of alcohol and other CNS depres- . Withdrawal symptoms have occurred following abrupt discontinuance. Keep tion-prone individuals under careful surveillance because of their predisposi- to habituation and dependence. In pregnancy, lactation or women of child- ng age, weigh potential benefit against possible hazard.
utions: If combined with other psychotropics or anticonvulsants, consider lly pharmacology of agents employed. Usual precautions indicated in patients ely depressed, or with latent depression, or with suicidal tendencies. Observe precautions in impaired renal or hepatic function. Limit dosage to smallest ve amount in elderly and debilitated to preclude ataxia or oversedation.
Effects: Drowsiness, confusion, diplopia, hypotension, changes in libido, nau- atigue, depression, dysarthria, jaundice, skin rash, ataxia, constipation, head- incontinence, changes in salivation, slurred speech, tremor, vertigo, urinary ion, blurred vision. Paradoxical reactions such as acute hyperexcited states, ty, hallucinations, increased muscle spasticity, insomnia, rage, sleep distur- s, stimulation, have been reported; should these occur, discontinue drug. Iso- reports of neutropenia, jaundice; periodic blood counts and liver function tests ible during long-term therapy.

Valium® **(diazepam)**

1g, 5-mg, 10-mg tablets

help relieve psychic tension I its somatic symptoms

and feel their rights are not equal, because I would not trust some of these women with making any decision that would affect my life.

I had a great fear of becoming like them. After all, I too had nothing to really care about other than knitting baby sweaters, planning the colour of the living room— tasks which don't matter to or impress anyone who visits. I did these things because I figured it made me happy, when actually it amused me only for a short time. Women do these little household frills only to affect a semblance of some change in their lives. To make their life a little brighter. But I did not want people to think I was stupid too, similar to the other women at the childbirth classes.

After my attack of nerves I started to think about my everyday situation, and tried to apply my feelings of anxiety to it. Things were bothering me, but I had never really analyzed them, until the following incident:

We grew more distant after the birth of our baby girl. He refused to share any responsibility in looking after her. While he was totally free to leave whenever he wished, I was encumbered with the obligation to find babysitters, make arrangements, get everything to- gether whenever I or we went out. I started to move further away from him after she was born.

For Tom, sex itself was a big thing. With me, sex is an emotional feeling, not so much a physical feeling. You don't manoeuvre someone into having an orgasm— it is emotional. If he can show me he loves me and I can show him I love him, then it works out right. But Tom was more bent on making me have orgasms. And if I didn't have one, he would become very upset. He continually joked about sex, constantly talked about getting into bed—at dinner, while relaxing in the living room. I got sick of it. He would always refer to going to bed, or mention funny remarks about different parts of my body, but not in a loving way.

In a sense I felt I was at his mercy. He was the man. He had the right to do what he wanted, not me. You are brought up to believe that the man fathers the family, and his wife makes him happy. For instance, in some women's magazines, you are instructed to do numerous things for him, to make him happy—and in turn maybe he will take you out to a movie for which you're supposed to be very thankful. A woman is not happy being protected, but then she needs to be pro- tected, so what else will she do? She's in a bind, a double bind.

I went into hysterics one night and he told me to shut up and went back to sleep. I was screaming and crying for hours with him continually yelling at me, "Why don't you shut up!" I sat out on the couch for the rest of the night by myself thinking. I was afraid of bothering him but at the same time I was frantic and

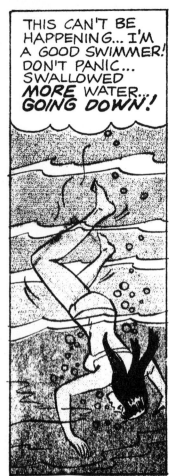

Reprinted through courtesy of **I Love You** Comic Magazine.

had to talk to him. But he continued to ignore me the entire night. I felt sometimes that what I thought, and what I did, were two different things. During a screaming fit I'd say in words what I thought, but actually feel otherwise inside. If I were screaming he would think I was having a tantrum. I couldn't communicate my frustration and need to him. He would simply think I was having a fit, when I was really not.

Frustration caused the hysteria. But I didn't understand that either. It just happened. I was just so lost and disgusted, wanted to hit anything in sight, throw everything around, stomp on things—just to release the frustration.

I also felt very afraid of hurting him at this time or have him lose his love for me and hurt me back or say: "You really aren't worth it anymore so let's go our own separate ways." No woman wants to have a man walk out on her, say they are finished. I didn't want him to finish the relationship because that would have put me right down to where I was before—no feeling of being somebody at all. Because before I really was nothing, I was there for them to do what they wanted with me. I had to be thankful that I had this much. So I was constantly afraid that if I asserted my temper, or really put my position, that, quite frankly, he would leave.

But it got to the point where I didn't see any purpose to our relationship. At first my purpose was—we'll get married, have a house, have his children, do things together, I'll look after the house and children, we'll go through the whole cycle. My role was to make his life happy—that was my purpose. But I finally came to notice that he really didn't care about me. He thought about himself and didn't want me to leave him because of his own comfort and ego, but he did not care about my feelings at all. I saw near the end that I had no purpose at all in being in that situation.

I had begun to develop some sense of self-confidence. During the last year of our marriage I began to study at night school. My first purpose was only to achieve some contact with people and something outside of my home—but as I learned I started feeling that I had capabilities. I started feeling like I was someone too. This was my first burst of confidence. After I wrote a few exams (I'd never achieved in school before), people started advising me to get work in drafting, work I was qualified for in jobs that women rarely do. It was certainly not the typical clerk-typist role. I was being challenged.

Whereas previously I had felt I was nothing, my new ambitions and study gave me great confidence. I began to respect myself, feel I could rely on myself. My husband had always been my support—the only thing that held me up. But near the end I was much more confident in speaking the truth to him because I knew I could look out for myself. I didn't fear risking his displeasure because I knew I didn't need his pleasure to exist by. Now I knew I could look out for myself. And I'm doing that now.

My child and I live alone. I am working, I am proud of my ability to support us, and I have now begun a beautiful relationship with another man.

I think I will eventually get married again and have more children—but I shall always keep my interest and activity in my chosen field. I shall always have to have something of my own. I remember when people used to come over to visit Tom and me. They would always talk about what he had done. They always addressed me as Mrs. Cooper, not Christine. "How's your wife these days" was as far as their concern for wives went. When men talk, they never talk about their wives doing anything. It is always what the guy is doing. But I got sick of being called Tom's wife. I was myself. I had feelings, I did things, I had reasons. Now I'm not called Tom's wife. People speak to me as an individual. I'm Christine.

Motherhood

Motherhood is the point at which many women falter. In a sense it is a point of no return, of unretractable commitment. One cannot divorce a child; nor can one divorce one's body and spirit from the being that grows inside. Norman Mailer even suggests that woman is "a privileged element of nature, closer to the mysteries than men". But such a view is highly romanticized, unfair to man and misleading to woman. For although woman may appear to be closer to the mysteries, she is not as close as she would like to be. Even though she possesses the source of creation, that source remains inside her; its wonderful presence is still infuriatingly distant, untouchable by the possessor. A woman's self-perception stands awed yet confounded before what Mailer terms "the mysterious advantage and burden of her womb".

Woman falters here, not because children prevent her from exploring her destiny, but because of her enormous difficulty in seeing clearly her role in childbirth and motherhood. She gloriously but perplexedly embodies "the connection between all things", while she herself is excluded from that connection. She contains the connection but is not the connection.

Just as between man and woman there are veils that impede understanding, there are also veils between a woman's self and her role as a procreator and mother. Until very recently women accepted the masks or stereotypes of motherhood, but now they are struggling to burst through them and discover their unique selves. In order to do that, they must first be able to identify the stereotypes, the Mother Myths. That is the purpose of this chapter—to throw into relief the mythic images of woman-as-mother by talking to several women about their actual experiences of motherhood, from their reasons for having children to their accounts of pregnancy, birth, childbearing, and their status as mothers.

Woman's search for self-definition is a major motive for having babies. In this chapter one woman talks about having a child to banish her insecurity as a female, while another admits she had nothing else to do at the time. For yet another, maternity was accidental; only one woman regarded it as a separate joy. With all these women, however, expectations of motherhood were influenced by external mother-images, and differed greatly from the reality that was eventually experienced. As one woman says, "I had considered motherhood as a state of being; I now realize it is merely a task."

These women express very different reactions to being pregnant; some were elated and joyful, others extremely depressed. The very nature of pregnancy is ambivalent, as Simone de Beauvoir points out in *The Second Sex*: "Caught up in the great cycle of the species, she affirms life in the teeth of time and death; in this she glimpses immortality . . . this projection of herself is also for the woman the foreshadowing of her death." Not only do women feel the life-death conflict in birth, but, as many of the women interviewed describe, the conflict between possessing and being possessed by the newborn child. Also difficult to contend with are the varying reactions of husbands to the double-image of the pregnant woman—at the same time beautiful and ugly.

Motherhood is advertised in women's magazines and other cultural forms as the happy pinnacle of the female condition. Yet so many are depressed after giving birth; so many experience "post-partum blues". Here depression is caused by the physical shock and exhaustion itself, but it is compounded by anxiety resulting from the fact that our culture rarely admits to the existence of unhappy mothers. Mothers are expected to be joyfully fulfilled by childbirth, but, as one woman in the chapter explains, she was not—and her depression turned to desperation because she felt her feelings were abnormal, when in fact they were shared by many other women. It is this kind of stereotype that must be shattered before woman can choose motherhood honestly and freely.

Few of the women speaking in this chapter were totally satisfied by bearing and raising children. Many felt constricted and frustrated during a life phase that is supposed to lead women along a path to completeness. During the 1940s and 50s motherhood became a cult, whose members devoted themselves to extolling the aesthetics of childbirth and breastfeeding as high culture. But are the proponents of the motherhood cult merely *powerless* people trying to appear powerful by sheer weight of numbers? Motherhood, it could be said, is a cult by default rather than decision.

Women form a subculture in society. The basic component is mother and daughters. Add to that a few cousins, aunts and grandma and you've got a genuine culture. But of course society does not recognize this subculture. It is a secret society except without the imbued mystique of an organization like the Freemasons or the Church. It produces its own syndrome and momentum.

That is why mothers pressure their daughters to have children as soon as possible. It brings more people into this subculture, and thus helps truly helpless, powerless people to feel more powerful.

From "Motherhood is Where It's At"
Produced for the C.B.C. by
Gail Dexter and Paulette Jiles

One belief that is mercifully dying out is the religious mystique of maternity as a justification for sex—the biblical message of St. Paul to all those who still believe in woman's payment for original sin: ". . . but the woman being deceived was in the transgression. Notwithstanding she shall be saved in childbearing" (Timothy 2:14-15). Let nothing more be said of that.

But still pervasive is the myth of pregnancy-as-painful-ordeal, perpetuated in a thousand old wives' tales and in the passage from Genesis that somberly intones "in sorrow thou shalt bring forth children". Several of the women here point out that childbirth can be beautiful and enjoyable: that agony is brought about through fear and ignorance. Natural childbirth can be pleasurable, they explain, if the medical bureaucracy complies with the mother's desire to give birth without anaesthetic, and if she has undergone instruction in the process of childbirth and techniques of breathing and muscle relaxation. One woman even describes an orgasm that she experienced at the moment of birth. But throughout the section dealing with birth in this chapter runs the theme of overbearing, repressive doctors representing a professional establishment that negates the needs and views of women; the mother is strapped down and drugged just at the moment when she might be experiencing one of the greatest moments of her life. Responsibility for birth has been taken, in a sense, out of the womb of the mother into the hands of the doctor, with resulting disillusionment.

Also discussed here is the nuclear-family-happily-ever-after myth. Several mothers discuss the isolation they feel in the small middle-class family setup and their attempts to find more creative alternatives for themselves and their children, such as co-operative day-care centres or communal living arrangements.

Most of the statements included in the following pages come from five women who were interviewed separately for this chapter. These fictitious names will identify each speaker:

Margaret: a thirty-year-old middle-class mother of two children, a university graduate who does not have a career but is involved in a co-operative day-care centre. Margaret is married to a man who supports her desire to develop her skills and talents beyond her role as mother and is sympathetic to the aims of the women's movement.

Sylvia: forty-eight, married, has two children, and is beginning a new career as an education consultant.

Eleanor: a twenty-year-old single girl who left home at the age of fifteen, lived with different men for a few years before settling with one with whom she had a baby, now a year old; she has since left her former lover and now lives with her child in a commune; she does not work but is considering a career as a physio-therapist.

Rachel: thirty-five, divorced and remarried with two children, a feminist, university graduate and librarian.

Virginia: twenty-one, now lives alone with her two-year-old child and works as a bookkeeper; comes from a poor working-class family from which she ran away at the age of fourteen. She married at seventeen and has since become divorced.

Our intention here was to make a random choice of individuals of various ages and backgrounds who would represent only their individual experiences. Neverthe-less, throughout the following pages run certain themes, producing an interwoven pattern of thought and feeling, a shared experience which, in a way, links all women as sisters.

Eleanor: *I was always unsure about being feminine. A baby, I hoped, would help me to understand myself as a woman. I did not get along with girlfriends; I felt very different from them. They played these little female games which didn't feel right. I became very insecure. What was it all about—being a woman. Being a mother would help me find out.*

Margaret: *I had nothing else to do! I had no alternative. I had graduated from university and couldn't throw myself into graduate school. I'd never worked and had never thought in terms of a career, and so I had no real skill or direction. And I loved kids. So I figured I might as well start the child thing. Now was as good a time as any.*

Eleanor: *I was searching for an honest relationship with someone. I had been on my own for a few years after leaving home at the age of fifteen. Living off the street, moving from place to place, man to man, I had never felt satisfied with my friendships. People were not being as sincere with me as I wanted to be with them. What I desired most was someone to comfort me, someone who would give to me without making me feel obligated. That's when I decided to have a baby.*

Margaret: *Children have normally borne the burden of the reinforcement of a marriage. That's a heavy trip!*

Rachel: *My first pregnancy was unwanted; but twelve years ago people didn't consider abortion that readily; if newly married, one was assumed to desire a family. But I had many misgivings. I was not prepared to be a mother. I worried: "What will I do?" "How will I handle the baby?" Also, I couldn't imagine that I would love* this *thing,* suddenly *just because it popped out of me.*

Margaret: *Motherhood is mysterious and beautiful but it is not essential to my self-definition as a woman.*

Sylvia: *I married twenty-five years ago and my prime reason for doing so was to have children. I regarded pregnancy as very sexy and I looked forward, passionately, to having babies. To me, that seemed the most delightful idea possible. I never had any doubts but that I would do very well as a mother.*

Eleanor: *When I first became pregnant he was very upset. We had been living together for one year, he was supporting me, and we had both agreed on a child. But when it actually happened, he didn't want it; he asked me to get an abortion. But I was prepared to have this baby by myself if necessary. "I won't get rid of it just because you don't want it," I told him. "It's my baby. And I want it." That was the first time I went against his wishes. The child was the most important thing I had ever done in my life.*

Rachel: *My only positive thoughts were selfish. I imagined parading down the street with this beautifully dressed extension of myself by my side.*

Eleanor: *I wanted to give to a child everything my mother hadn't given me—honest love without demands. It wasn't important that the baby should have to love me in return. The important thing was having a new honest person with whom I could relate freely and someone who would accept me as I was, with no pre-conceived notion about what I should be. If he were to give me anything he would do so because he wanted to, not because I expected it.*

Margaret: *When I learned the rabbit test was positive I didn't feel trapped but fated. I had absolutely no choice but at the end of nine months—whoosh, I would be a mother. My fate had never been that definite, so determined—and that terrified me.*

John Phillips

She feels it as at once an enrichment and an injury; the fetus is part of her body, and it is a parasite that feeds on it; she possesses it, and she is possessed by it; it represents the future, and, carrying it, she feels herself vast as the world; but this very opulence annihilates her, she feels that she herself is no longer anything. A new life is going to manifest itself and justify its own separate existence, she is proud of it; but she also feels herself tossed and driven, the plaything of obscure forces.

Simone de Beauvoir
The Second Sex

Eleanor: *Being pregnant, I felt secure within myself for the first time in my life. I was really thrilled. Every day I would stand in front of the mirror to see how much my belly had grown. To me my body was so beautiful. I was proud to finally walk down the street with a huge stomach.*

Rachel: *I hated it. Pregnancy was deforming, not physically but psychologically. That entity growing inside felt more unnatural than natural. I was stuffed up and couldn't breathe with this thing jammed into my innards. I loathed my first pregnancy so much that I used to stand in front of the mirror and beat my belly yelling: "I hate this, I hate it, I hate it."*

It was strange to see my beautiful marble body softened and broken and stretched and deformed. . . . Where was my lovely, youthful Naiad form? Where my ambition? My fame? . . . This game with the giant Life was too much. But then I thought of the child to come, and all such painful thoughts ceased. . . . Cruel hours of tender waiting in the night. . . . With what a price we pay for the glory of motherhood.

Isadora Duncan
My Life

Eleanor: *He found my pregnancy and big belly disgusting. He was repelled by my changing figure more than anything else. To him a pregnant woman was an ugly woman. It was summertime and when we went out walking he would point out how great other chicks looked parading down the street. Around my fourth month he stopped sleeping with me. Finally the point arrived when if he wanted to sleep with someone else, someone he found more attractive because they were not pregnant, I resigned myself to that. But I felt very ugly, very unattractive in his eyes. I felt very strange, conflicting emotions at that time. For a while I got into really hating myself, hating my pregnancy, and feeling repulsive. Yet at the same time I was very proud of myself. I knew this baby was important and right. Only around him did I feel self-disgust.*

He became more and more distant. I kept hoping his attitude would change; I tried to interest him in the coming baby but he continued to draw away. Most of the time he tried to ignore the fact that I was pregnant. It took until the eighth month before he would even touch my stomach, to feel the baby kicking. It frightened him, I think. He was so afraid he didn't want to have anything to do with it. I do not understand his fear even now when I think back.

Virginia: *My husband showed no interest in the birth of our baby. He was not even at the hospital while she was being born. He was convinced that childbearing was a woman's job. "Your body forms the baby," he told me. "You have the capability of delivering it; you are the one who is supposed to be in the labour room, not me." In his view the father had nothing to do with childbirth. "While you're in the hospital having the baby," he said, "I'll be at the local bar having a beer."*

Margaret: *I started an ongoing battle with my obstetrician for natural childbirth. I wanted to fight the professional medical view of childbirth as illness. At first the doctor agreed to my request. But by the seventh month he was equivocating, and at the eighth he said: "If you really feel that way about having children why don't you go to the Polynesian islands and have it in the bushes the way the natives do?" What does one do at that point?*

I had been directed to a hospital known to tolerate natural childbirth. But the system was set up for passive birth and the exercises prescribed by my doctor were not actual natural-childbirth ones; consequently, I was not prepared for what happened.

My husband was allowed into the delivery room only after a fight with the doctor. Thank God he was there. First there was the shock of lying on this metal table, hips strung up in the air, arms and wrists tied to poles. I remember screaming: "Don't do this, I can't work in this position. I cannot push a baby out with my feet up in the air." But of course they would not unstrap me. It was a battle. I felt I was constantly struggling, battling contrary forces. The machinery was geared to passive childbirth and worked against my attempts to deliver naturally. It was tough. My only wish was to survive through it. While sewing me up I remember the doctor muttering, "It wouldn't have been this bad, if you had not insisted on the natural way." My last thought was: "I've blown my guts out."

Virginia: *Before the birth of my second baby I attended a government health-department class for pregnant women (not a natural-childbirth class). That was a great mistake. I trusted that a government programme would offer good down-to-earth advice for women. But the instructor was unqualified and ignorant herself. She was also condescending and put most of us women down. She also scared a lot of women by exaggerating the pain of childbirth. Never having experienced childbirth herself, she exaggerated the pain to the point where many women in the class were terrified as their time drew near.*

Women have to be informed by others about what to expect, but they must be properly prepared. There is no need for fear. Birth is so very natural; yet so many are frightened. And the greater the fear, the greater the pain. Not once did our instructor even hint that giving birth may in some way be enjoyable. She stressed that the product—the baby—was wonderful, but that the actual delivery was an unfortunately lamentable experience one had to go through.

I remember going on a group tour to preview the hospital. When we arrived at the delivery room several women immediately became hysterical. Everyone is brought up to believe that having a baby is supposed to be painful.

Pregnant animals of all kinds have a powerful "nesting instinct" which earlier in pregnancy makes them create a hiding place of the greatest possible security where they will go to have the baby when it comes. Yet human mothers are forced to leave the security of their nest, their home, and go off to a strange building full of sterile furnishings and sterile people. . . . Her husband isn't allowed to be with her. The husband gets frustrated. The woman gets frantic, she panics at the slightest of labour contractions. She is sedated and starts having nightmares. The contractions strengthen and she totally freaks out, becoming violent. She is strapped down and on her back, which is not necessarily the position a woman will assume for birth if it is left up to her. She is terrified and highly uncomfortable, physically, because she can't change positions. She tightens her body out of fear and that increases the pain of the contractions. She screams out in terror. A calm-voiced anaesthetist smiles down into her face and asks if she wants something to "take the edge off". She says yes and in a few minutes is drugged into complete unconsciousness. Since she can't push any more the doctor has to pull the baby out by the head with forceps, a more dangerous procedure than normal expulsion. When the mother awakes an hour or so later she is extremely sick to her stomach from the drugs and her baby is nowhere in sight. . . . The whole thing is a comedy of errors except that it isn't very funny. Most of the problems and discomforts of childbirth are totally creations of hospitals.

Laura Jones and John Phillips
from This Magazine is About Schools

Rachel: *The doctor did not believe me during my second pregnancy when I insisted the child was to be born soon. From my first experience I knew the symptoms exactly. I remember calling him when my water had already broken, and contractions were every three minutes. I told him the child was coming within hours. "Oh no dear, that's impossible; you don't know what you're talking about." He saw me at his office, made me climb up on a table (I had a pencil between my teeth because of the pain), examined me, then suddenly jumped back because the head was already there. He got two people to assist me down, when two minutes previously he had forced me to climb up myself. I was rushed to the hospital, I ran up three flights of stairs because of a late elevator, and was left in the prep room, where the nurses moved lackadaisically. I urged them to hurry, yelled repeatedly "The baby is being born," but "No honey, don't worry about it," was the reply. They treat pregnant women in this ridiculously childish manner. Some nurse got very mad saying "Look, we're doing our job here, you don't know what you're talking about." At this point the doctor rushed in and gave them hell. The baby's head was already pushing through. Just as they rolled me into the operating room, the baby was born. No one had done anything. God, they are such a bunch of stupid asses. I may not be a physician or nurse but I knew what was happening in my own body. But they don't give a shit about that. They totally negate your feelings.*

Margaret: *I was properly prepared in natural childbirth for my second child. The difference was phenomenal. This time the process and I were in harmony. I knew what was happening. Without understanding the process of birth, you become quite terrorized by the power of your own body. It becomes quite alien from you because you're using muscles that have never been used before, with a strength you have never felt at any other time. It is a supernatural kind of force that you produce and it is fantastically strange if you have not consciously worked your body towards this point, mind and body in harmony.*

To be crouched back, watching this thing happen, is a frightful experience because the force is so totally polarized. You are passive but your body is extremely active. But when you're in control you become suddenly aware of participating in an extremely powerful activity —something greater than yourself. There is a huge mystery in childbirth—you are taking part in the power of creation. If you are in rhythm with your body, the experience is exhilarating. It is the most natural event and we have made it the most alien.

John Phillips

. . . the more civilised the people, the more the pain of labour appears to become intensified.

Grantly Dick Read
Childbirth Without Fear

Sylvia: *When I gave birth to my second child I had what amounted to the greatest orgasm of my life. But at the time I was so shocked by it, because I had never heard of such a sensation associated with birth, that I was too embarrassed to talk or even think about it. Years later I discussed it with a doctor who said he had encountered a few such experiences, and that according to medical literature, women should be experiencing more sexual and sensual feelings at childbirth. But most doctors and women rarely think about birth in a sensual way at all. There's a real physical pleasure in having a child along with the pain; somewhere along the line our culture has forgotten this.*

Rachel: *I remember how shocked I was, even though the experience was not terribly painful. My knees were shaking and I was scared, very scared. Labour pains had taken over and my body was completely beyond my control—I was an extension, something out there beyond, a baby-making machine. And the machine had taken over, the machine was going to spew this thing out. No, I really did not feel that great moment of closeness. I was simply relieved that the thing was at last out of me. . . .*

My husband was not there but I was just as glad. Even today, twelve years later, I would feel strange about having him present, except perhaps to understand what a woman goes through in childbirth, so he would think more seriously about birth control or vasectomy. Some women say it is romantic to be together at the time of birth, but quite frankly while a man has a hell of a lot of responsibility, let's face it—his role ends at the moment of conception. Unfortunately that is the way it is. I am the producer, the baby producer. . . .

Childbirth is a private affair. I would have preferred to go in a corner somewhere to deliver the baby by myself without doctors and nurses around. I hated the open operating theatre where everyone watched as I lay spreadeagled, legs in stirrups, exposed like a strip dancer.

Margaret: *As soon as the baby had left my body it was another person—I did not feel this cosmic tie of the body. It could have been someone else's baby. Even as I was leaving the hospital I was not familiar with the child. Its dependency was not obvious at that stage. It was a little stranger.*

Rachel: *Horror was my first reaction to seeing the baby at birth. It was covered in mucous and blood and was worse than any animal I had ever seen. My only concern was its sex and its health. Was it all right? I couldn't imagine that it was, all gnarled and ugly.*

Goo-goo, coo-coo, sweet-little-baby-family-forever lovely—I did not feel that. Instead I thought: "It's a thing, a small thing, I have to care for it, I am responsible. And wow, I can hardly wait until it is old enough for day-care, so that I can do something meaningful with my life." . . .

Did I have post-partum blues! At the time I didn't know what it was, that many other women felt the same way. I thought I was going insane or having a nervous breakdown. I cried, felt depressed, the world had ended, and yet here I was supposed to be having this idyllic experience in motherhood, if you believe the magazines.

I hated being in the house. I longed for contact, intellectual stimulation. In between bathing the baby, which was fun, I read, took walks, wrote letters, but I was damned bored. Mothers are supposed to feel this great surge of satisfaction from nursing, feeding, and rearing their kids, but I just never felt that way. I didn't dislike this thing but somehow I could not think of it at first as a child, a family member—until it grew. By three months I started to feel love for it—but not mother love. I was not a natural mother. And at that time I felt very guilty about it. But having talked to many other women since, I've found that reaction to be not unusual.

. . . the first thing she does (every morning) is put the bacon on and the water for coffee. Then she goes back to her room and makes up the bed. . . . By that time the pan is hot and she runs back to turn the bacon. She finishes making the children's breakfast and she is lucky she gets to serve it before she is forced to dash off and attend to the baby, changing him, and sitting him up. She rushes back, plops him in a little canvas chair, serves the children if she has not already done so, and makes her husband's breakfast. And so it goes through the day. . . . It's like watching the old-time movie in which for technical reasons everyone seems to be moving at three times normal speed. In this case it is not so funny.

Beverly Jones
"The Dynamics of Marriage and Motherhood"
Sisterhood is Powerful

Margaret: *I was very close to my first child because all this surplus energy, previously directed into studying, friends, or social-political activities, now zeroed in on this little infant.*

That's too great a burden for a child. It was a fairly intense relationship. We spent most of every day together and I began to see things through child's eyes and experienced the joy of reliving childhood through him. But as he got older the relationship became suffocating for both of us. He was limited to where he could go, and I had no other place (like a day nursery) to turn to during that period. When he was eighteen months old I could no longer stimulate him. He was bored with me. He would destroy things because he had played out everything in the house. We had made the rounds of all the local parks, all the garbage cans in the lanes—but what we both really required was socializing with other people.

You see this so clearly in the parks. The faces. The mothers just limply walking beside the kid, staring blankly. I did that. A terrific amount of energy is repressed there. At one point it became frightening because I knew exactly how to manipulate him. He was a marionette, and so was I. We manipulated each other because our direction was pointed inward toward ourselves, not outward toward a community.

Rachel: *Motherhood as natural is a myth, I now feel. The tie with the body is not important. Had I adopted a child at one week or ten days, the experience would be the same, because my child didn't become a person for me until after a few months.*

After the fourth month I had to find a job. My husband went off to work every day. And stuck in the house my only anticipation was for this adult to come home every night and talk to me. By the fifth month I had a job and a good babysitter.

Margaret: *Dumping him on a babysitter was simply running away from the problem. Also I had nothing I could do, no skill, no career training. Where would I go if I went out of the house!*

Rachel: *Staying at home I would have been a picky, nagging, nervous, upset mother. My child would have developed a hell of a lot of problems. As it was he had an earth-mother-type babysitter who performed all the motherly tasks I could not do, or was not prepared to do. And I offered him something completely different—a relationship on another level. And he accepted me for myself. Sure I was a little guilty, especially if he were sick, but that was the price I paid. I could not have managed any other way, especially as the child grew older. I looked forward to seeing him when I returned home at night, and enjoyed him thoroughly on weekends. This way I knew I would be a better mother and my child a healthier person. My husband (divorced, I'm now remarried) did not disagree with my working because he liked the extra money. But at the time of divorce he told a marriage counsellor I was not a good mother and should have remained at home. He never said that to me during our marriage; but even if he had, I would have done what I did.*

Eleanor: *I thought conditions between him and me would change after the baby's birth. But even though he did like the child, he still did not want me as a person, as a woman. Even though my figure came back, to him I was still heavy, ugly, homely. And yet I wasn't. During the pregnancy I had thought that my physical state was what had really bothered him. Obviously it was not just that. There was a lot more to it. But even now I am not sure about what actually happened and why.*

Virginia: *If I went out to the store he would beg me to hurrry back—he did not want to be alone with the baby, his baby. I realized finally that he was afraid of her. If I went out I had to struggle to obtain a babysitter, make arrangements—he did nothing. And yet he did not understand what I was going through.*

Eleanor: *I have never considered him as* my *baby. He's just a little person whom I have to help along for a while until he is capable of making his own decisions. I do not want to impose anything upon him. He needs me for the basic necessities—food, love, security. I've never thought of him as an extension of myself, as I understand many other mothers do. He is a complete individual. He is my child just because I am his mother. Otherwise he is his own.*

Margaret: *We live in the isolation of the typical nuclear family. When we are alone in our ten-room house in the winter we relate to few other people and so have nothing to give each other. We feed on one another and begin to destroy one another. The nuclear family of parents and children has become a demonic institution.*

It is as if we took the yolk from an egg, discarded the shell and egg white, and were surprised to find it didn't become a healthy chick. The nuclear family has become the basic economic unit of our society—one house, one washing machine, one car. It has eliminated natural co-operation among relatives and neighbours and instead constructed a barrier to extra-family relations.

The isolation which makes the red-brick-villa household so neurotic did not exist [in feudal times]. There was friction but it had no chance to build itself into the intense, introverted anguish of the single eye-to-eye confrontation of the isolated spouses.

Germaine Greer
The Female Eunuch

Margaret: *With my second child I made a conscious move to belong to a community, and became involved in a co-operative half-day nursery. The nursery has evolved to the point where only two parents a day are required at the school. But even now there are still guilt feelings connected with this arrangement. We have to find an alternative to the institutional day-care centre, one that is a genuine familial environment, before we can feel free to leave our children.*

Eleanor: *I thought of taking him to a day-care centre but I do not trust other people—strangers—enough. There are so many restrictions and values that people impose upon children unknowingly or unthinkingly. I'd much rather continue with what I am doing now—taking him to friends whom I trust not to confuse him or be dishonest with him. People in centres may be fine—but they are still strangers whose ideas I do not know. And I fear that they may repress him.*

Rachel: *Each time the kids become more independent, I become more involved with them—when they are not depending on me for services they're depending on me in another, warmer, closer way.*

Now we share ideas and feelings instead of routine incidentals. Each time my children grow they become more interesting to me. I feel they will be at their most interesting as full adults. And I look forward to the day. That is when I feel the relationship will be best.

Eleanor: *My child needs to be around other women and men. I do not want to be the only woman he is close to. My parents were very protective with me and consequently I was never with other adults. From the day my son was one week old I decided we could not make it alone as a neat little family. I want to be honest and not lay my impressions on him but I know that is in a sense impossible. That will happen simply because I am there. This is why it is important for him to associate with many different kinds of people in different environments, so that he can see for himself that people differ. Hopefully when he is old enough to choose, he can then choose freely for himself. I do not want him to grow up in my fantasy world or the fantasy world of others. I want him to have a realistic view of life.*

Sylvia: *Today we don't have children in the large household or village atmosphere that existed for hundreds of years before us. We do not have the feeling of bringing up our children according to how our mothers brought us up, or how our grandmothers brought them up. We are trying to forge our own way, and we're ignoring, fighting tradition. That is very frightening. We turn to our peers, our contemporaries, our friends. But it's scary to be out there on the edge, and yet right now how do we bring up our kids for the 1990s? We just don't know what is going to happen.*

Rachel: *I tried following the advice of popular child-psychologists but found them useless. I remember reading the advice of one expert who described a situation where the child became very angry with his mother for not preparing his lunch on time. The psychologist suggested: "Don't get mad, apologize to the child, and make the lunch immediately." My son read this too, and asked: "Mom, why didn't he tell that mother to just say 'Get your ass into the kitchen and make your own goddamned lunch.' "*

I am rarely inhibited emotionally in front of my children. I am just too honest. I tried this phony, let's-not-argue-in-front-of-the-children tactic but found it impossible. Anger and release are part of life. Our fighting concerns the kids; but at the same time we'd be very dishonest to have our children think that people live happily ever after without friction.

Some of my friends are appalled by my attitude. They consider it very damaging. And yes, my children do get censured for the open manner by which we live. It has caused them problems because they do not live in a typical middle-class home. But the only way to get around that would be for their father not to have been a draft resister, their parents not to have been atheists, their mother not to have been divorced, their mother not to have been a feminist. We are not typical. And

the children suffer for it somewhat—but perhaps later
they would have suffered more for the other experience.

Eleanor: *The women's magazines hand down an image*
of the "Big M" Mother. Someone I don't want to be. She
is very repressive, very possessive, does not regard
her child as an individual, lays down expectations for
him—the big M Mother is merely substituting for her
own ambitions.

Rachel: *The motherhood cult does not interest me. I*
have nothing in common with someone just because she
is a mother. So many mothers say to me—"I don't know
how you do it, career plus children," as if it were beyond
them. I simply reply that I had no choice, because of the
type of person I am. I did it out of necessity. I must
admit I have put myself first. But only by placing myself
first can I be a good parent. I never make sacrifices and
so I'll never have to say to them: "Look how I sacrificed
for you," and they will never feel guilt for anything I
might have given up.

Margaret: *What do I have as a person who has gone*
through motherhood? A memory of a six-hour birth in
one case and a two-hour experience in another. Of
course I have two other people in my family but that is
not entirely satisfying from dawn to dusk—that's not
enough. What I really mean to say about motherhood in
the light of my six years of childrearing is: I see it not
as a state of being, but as a task. A task which I can
also share with non-mothers, women who are not baby
producers. It has taken me six years to see that the
raising of children is a task.

Rachel: *It's an administrative job. Household and child*
responsibilities are still mine even though my husband
is willing to share the work since I have a career as
well. He helps me but I am still the overseer. It's my
duty to check what has to be done. It is always done if
I ask—but why do I have to ask? To me that is a psycho-
logical load. By the way, every day it works better. My
husband (second husband) cares. We are getting there
slowly but it is in no way equal. And I don't know if it
ever can be, because men are just not socialized the
way we are.

Virginia: *I was twenty years old but I had lost touch*
with my generation. All my friends were in school,
working or travelling, while I was always with my baby
in this tiny apartment. They belonged to a youth culture
but I seemed to have missed all that. I jumped from
adolescence straight into middle age.

Margaret: *Lack of self-worth goes along with this situa-*
tion. All you have to offer at the end of the day are the
dishes you washed, the pants you changed, and the
flowers you saw on your walk. Meanwhile the father
is growing more involved daily in his activities as the
mother remains static and confined. He can afford to
enjoy the children because participation is on his terms.
So while the man becomes more alive the woman be-
comes more dead. Childrearing is a direct cause of that.

But in any case giving birth and suckling are not activi-
ties, they are natural functions; no project is involved;
and that is why woman found in them no reason for a
lofty affirmation of her existence—she submitted pas-
sively to her biological fate. The domestic labours that
fell to her lot because they were reconcilable with the
cares of maternity imprisoned her in repetition and
immanence . . . they produced nothing new.

Simone de Beauvoir
The Second Sex

Rachel: *If I were born in this generation I'd question*
very highly the value of having children. There is over-
population and plenty of children in this world already
who need love.

Eleanor: *I would love to be pregnant again even though*
I'm young and "unmarried", but I don't think I will. In a
sense it is a very unfair and selfish pre-occupation on
my part to want to bring up a child in this world which
is exploding all around us. I realize, on the other hand,
that it's bad for my child to grow up as an only child;
but then again we live in a community of people and he
is not alone. Things have a way of working themselves
out.

Rachel: *We are fast approaching a time, I hope, where*
the father takes on an emotional responsibility and
where the child is not dependent on two persons in a
nuclear family. If I were a young person today with the
opportunity to live amongst a group of people who
shared child responsibilities, it would be unnecessary
for me to be a mother. Kids are great but I could have
that involvement with other people's children.
    Sure my children add to my life now—but only be-
cause they are there. Believe me, if they weren't there
I would have moved in other directions, experimented
with different professions, or built a better relationship
with a man. These may be very selfish feelings; after all
I do not consider myself a "good" mother, but I think if I
had had the choice I would have left childbearing to
those women who really wanted to be mothers.

Laura Jones

John Phillips

Eleanor: I wanted to have a baby partly to find myself as a woman. I now feel that motive was neurotic. The baby taught me that. With him I have learned to give without getting from him a purpose for myself. By feeling for him I've learned to feel for other people without requiring from them an image of myself. Being honest with the baby I have tried not to lay my expectations on him. And I no longer anticipate the reverse—other people laying their expectations on me. I feel more in touch with myself now.

My baby has never prevented me from doing anything. The opposite is true. By having this child and this honest relationship with him, I have been impelled to recognize the myths others laid on me, the myths I laid on myself. Now I am discovering my own reality.

There is one more fiction that must be dealt with in any discussion of motherhood. In *The Baby Trap* by Ellen Peck, also the author of that classic *How to Get a Teenage Boy and What to Do With Him When You Get Him,* quoted in the chapter on socialization, children are blamed for catapulting wives and husbands into a nightmare of rigidity, boredom, loss of romance and confinement. Peck warns women about the dangers of having children: "There are other men . . . who find great satisfaction in the sense of personal power that comes from being able to buy whatever they want. They want their good scotch, stereo, vacation. They want a bright young thing on their arm (that's you) and that's that. Try to pin this sort of man down to a tight budget so that the kids can have everything from kiddie toys to college savings plans while he gives up his pleasures— and you've got trouble."

In other words, don't have kids because you won't be pleasing your man. This kind of male-gratifying argument is the same one that got women into *having* babies for the wrong reasons. The bait is the same: vulnerability, fear of abandonment, fear of self. Several women in this chapter did say that children prevented them from pursuing other objectives; another explained how the child opened up new realizations for her. But in each case it was not the child's mere presence that determined the situation—rather the woman's understanding (or lack of it) of why she had chosen motherhood.

Advice that rallies a woman to the support of her man's glamour-boy image denies both her dignity as a self-determining individual and her man's potential for fatherhood. Equally dangerous is the way it accounts for marital difficulties by discriminating against children, making them the scapegoats for estrangement between the sexes, for which the adults are in fact responsible.

In her essay, "The Institution of Sexual Intercourse",

radical feminist Ti-Grace Atkinson has gone even further in suggesting that women must be freed of the nine-months' encumbrance of pregnancy. "Sexual intercourse," she says, "would have to cease to be society's means to population renewal. This change is beginning to be within our grasp with the work now being done on extra-uterine conception and incubation. But the possibilities of this research for the woman's movement have been barely suggested and there would have to be very concentrated research to perfect development so that this could be a truly optional method, at the very least."

Perhaps this backlash against children was an inevitable reaction to years of uncritical acceptance of motherhood as the natural purpose of women: years in which the mythic image of the blissful mother obscured the real problems of pregnancy and maternity. An artificial womb may seem an attractive solution to the pregnant woman who is encouraged to feel ugly and embarrassed by her condition. But is the advice to shun pregnancy any more enlightened than urging her to hide her belly under petite frilly clothes? Both deny her sensual being, the vital and natural fact of her fertility.

The testimony of the women interviewed in these pages indicates that the burden of motherhood is not the child, but the lack of modern substitutes for (or improvements on) the support once provided by the extended family: grandmothers, aunts, grandfathers, uncles, brothers and sisters. Naturally if women continue to seek awareness of their own reality and break down the mystiques of motherhood, they will also have to explore creative alternatives to the raising of their children. A beginning is being made in this direction with the creation of day-care centres and communal living arrangements. But first must come awareness.

Consciousness Raising

The suffragettes united in a large body for political strength. They expected that the vote would be the key to a revolutionary change in the position of women in society; but time has contradicted them. They did not, as they had hoped, free the female from the restricting boundaries of "a woman's sphere". This is the task that remains today.

There are still political issues, such as equality in employment, abortion-law reform and the provision of a good day-care system, on which large groups of women are needed to press for change. But underlying these practical matters is the strong need for women to alter their view of themselves and each other. History has allowed us to see that this is the root of the problem.

Today's women's movement began with the idea of forming organizations on a mass scale. Many of these groups have since broken apart—partly because of the inevitable differences of approach that spring up in any large movement, but also because women are finding it more effective to work in small collectives on particular projects: day-care centres, birth-control and abortion counselling services, well-baby clinics, newspapers. But another activity, fundamental to the movement and to women's rediscovery of themselves, is the process of "consciousness raising", where small groups of women share their experiences, emotions and aspirations in a frank and personal way.

This chapter contains the transcript of a consciousness-raising session of a feminist group. It illustrates how the process enables women to vent their feelings with a large degree of honesty, so that they can attempt to deal with the contradictions of their lives, among which they often flounder in isolation. But even here, it becomes apparent that there are no clear-cut or easy answers. The group can be a supportive start for what must ultimately be individual decisions, even compromises.

An important aspect of these sessions is that the participants begin to understand that many of their personal problems are not as unique as they had thought, and are, to some extent, a product of their female conditioning. Another effect of the meetings is that women learn that they can like other women, that they need not be in competition with each other, that women are not inferior company to men. Eventually, perhaps, they will be able to work with one another in more externally focused projects, or have the strength to go out on their own in the world, or make difficult changes in their lives.

One can see in this group, composed of both old and new members, a collective pressure that pushes some into accepting positions of which they are not fully convinced. Clearly some of the women are stronger than the others; while they have escaped the intimidating presence of men by barring them from their meetings, they themselves may inadvertently be playing out a power game.

Airing past injuries and releasing years of pent-up hostility towards men can be healthy. (We have seen in the chapters "Women Through the Eyes of Others" and "Sexuality" that men have few inhibitions about giving vent to their hostility towards women.) But there is an attempt on the part of some members to foster a bitter attitude towards "men" in general, as expressed, for example, by the woman who says, "What could be worse than living with a man!" This view leads some to a position of lesbianism by ideology, as opposed to natural inclination. Or perhaps it is a rationalization for the latter.

Although this is one pitfall of the movement, we must affirm the fact that we have profited greatly from many of the insights shared at meetings such as these, where women struggle to deal honestly with their feelings—no matter how difficult it is to face up to what those feelings really mean, and despite the fact that one may have to reassess one's life in the light of those discoveries.

Kathy: *Did anyone come in here with doubts about feminism or were you already sold on all its tenets? Because I'm really in a conflict stage right now.*

Helene: *Well, the thing that brought me into feminism was that it clicked with my great long fight for identity. I've been fighting and didn't know what it was. And then, when I went to a feminist lecture I thought, wow, that's what I've been fighting about. I was told that's why you bleach your hair and that's why you wear lashes. It's all props for insecurity. But then I heard "Hate men". Well, my whole life has been geared to men. So, I figured there's got to be a way of doing it with them. Then I found out there is no way. You've got to do it by yourself. And then, in a couple of hundred years, when they get on to what we're talking about. . . .*

Kathy: *But was there anything positive in your life with men when you came in?*

Helene: *Yes, there was something positive. One thing. I knew that my father, absolutely from the first day, put me down.*

Kathy: *I wouldn't call that positive.*

Betty: *Are you implying, Kathy, that we're all a bunch of frustrated females that are here to. . . .*

Kathy: *No. Why did you come? Not to hate.*

Helene: *No, love. Love for myself. I'm not a destructive person. There is one thing that I found really positive. If there's one thing that feminists will have in the world it's truth and honesty between people. This is surely what we're after. This is the first thing that clicked in my head. I've heard the word truth and I've heard honest, but I didn't know what it meant until I got more and more into feminism. That surely was the first positive thing I realized. That's what we're after. Now, how can we be laughed at and put down for that.*

Kathy: *Well, I came in because of this man I was dating this past winter. This role-playing prevented me from really having a good relationship with him. I really couldn't get to know him because of this role-playing. I was told when we get married, you're going to do this, when I get married my wife will be this. And damn it all, I hated this because. . . .*

Helene: *You found yourself in a real put-down situation.*

Kathy: *But, Helene, it's also destroying him. He could be a real person.*

Helene: *The hell with him. It's you. . . .*

Kathy: *I'm not saying the hell with him. I happen to love him.*

Helene: *If you want something positive, love yourself. That's positive. That's bloody positive. Love yourself and get around to what's good for you.*

Kathy: *Well, I happen to care for another person. Does anybody else here care for another person?*

Helene: *Kathy, how do you figure you got the way you are. How do you figure your boyfriend has got that way.*

Phyllis: *You're putting yourself in the position that women always put themselves in of having to patch things up. Always having to think of other people. You're saying that you're really more concerned with helping this man than you are concerned about helping yourself.*

Kathy: *I'm concerned about the two of us together.*

Helene: *You're no good to anyone else until you're positive about yourself, until you can function on your own. What are you going to give him? Unless you've got something you can't give something.*

Sue: *You know, when I was a student in college I was engaged to this boy and he was president of this and president of that. He really had a lot to offer. He was a very intelligent person. But then I came to discover that he didn't want an equal partner. He wanted someone to cook for him and take care of him. It just ate him up that I'm a musician. He'd come at me sometimes and say, the only thing you can do is play the piano, but you can't cook. And I just sort of realized that he was going to put me in this little closet. I loved him but I couldn't take it.*

Betty: *There's always the male put-down, the male ego. The assumption that the happiest women are the women at home, the women who accept their roles and accept their femininity. The rest of us, we're just frustrated bitches.*

Helene: *The other night this guy said that the women who are carrying on, the feminists, are doing it because they are frustrated and have personal hangups. And they're so ugly they can't get married. I mean, nobody has ever said to this guy that the reason he's saying that is because he's physically inadequate.*

Carol: *He's got a small prick.*

Helene: *Yah, he's got a small prick. Now, no one has ever said that. But when a woman gets out and says I don't like it, automatically she's frustrated and has personal hangups. You're damned right we're frustrated and have personal hangups. And you know where we got them.*

Carol: *Damn right we're bitter. We have good reason for being bitter.*

Phyllis: *What really bothers me right now, what's really bugging me is why do we always wind up talking about men. I mean that's what our lives have been all about. We're still living through men. I mean, men are very important, children are important, but I really think our whole lives we think about men—our bosses, our husbands, our lovers—how to please them. I really think it's important for us to talk about ourselves and what happens inside us.*

Betty: *How do we get out from under?*

Sue: *We're doing it, aren't we?*

Irene: *We're doing it as a group.*

Phyllis: *We're reinforcing each other, for one thing. Every time we go to a meeting, every time we talk about it, we realize that it is a political thing. These aren't personal problems at all.*

Sue: *That's right. That's right. It's meant to be therapy in a sense, at first, when you first become conscious of it. It can be therapy until you start synthesizing your own thoughts about it and applying it to the political system, which seems to be the system of how can you please a man.*

Betty: *It seems to me when I was growing up, it was not considered a very good idea to have really close girl-friends. My mother always encouraged that one had boyfriends. And my husband didn't even like close girlfriends. You know, any problems that I had he felt I should be able to discuss with him. And I felt, and still feel, that men isolate women. You're isolated at home which really prevents you from getting together as a group. I think marriage does this.*

Phyllis: *I know I've always felt that I was being disloyal. For example, if you have a problem and you do think it's personal—for years I thought my problems were entirely personal and something I should work out myself —I think you are taught that if you talk about the problems with other people you're not being loyal to your family. Consequently, when you get together with a group of women you may allude to certain things but you never say anything that would be detrimental to your mate. You wouldn't want to bring any sort of harm to your relationship, and so you're loyal. So one good thing about getting together with a group like this for me was to find out that my problems were not personal at all. Every woman—and it just grows and grows as I read more and talk to more people and am not afraid to be open—every woman has experienced the same thing. You know, when you speak to the number of women that have been sexually abused by men you find almost all have. The number who have been physically abused by men, the number who have been just sort of cut off where the man doesn't communicate with you, this type of thing. You find that this is not personal. This is what we all experience. Out of this comes the political thing. You realize that it's not you who are inadequate, it's not just you who have a bad self-image. Women generally are just raised to have no identity. And we punish ourselves throughout life thinking this suffering is personal when it isn't.*

Irene: *Yes, you feel guilty. Guilty as hell all the time.*

Phyllis: *All the time. And what are you guilty about? You're guilty because you're a woman really, because you're nothing.*

Helene. And *it's always your fault. The minute you admit that something is wrong, you have to admit that you did it. What really amazes me is that when somebody finds out that you're a feminist they immediately say, "Well, I'm not." But then you start talking and they'll say, "Wait a minute. I never thought of that. That just happened to me."*

Phyllis: *Even if you know for sure it wasn't your fault, you have to say I'm sorry. You have to make up. Because as a woman our role is that of peacemaker. It's the woman's role to make sure the family is harmonious and smooth. All of us sitting at the table and smiling, you know, even if the guy's a bastard, you have to pretend that it's really a great deal.*

Helene: *And you know why. He just goes off, and there you are with the kids and the dishes. He doesn't have to talk to you. He's gone all day, he comes home and hides behind the paper. He knows that you are going to do it all. You'll make sure that the children don't notice that there's unrest there. He is free to go off and do what he likes and he's got you trapped. You have to rise to the occasion. All your life they've been preparing you to get this guy. You're being prepared to be pretty, for instance, pretty for a man. That's part of the service area too, not just washing dishes.*

Irene: *Look what happens to young girls. I was talking to a girl of about eighteen and she says, "Oh, but I really like being a sex object, don't you." She was talking about* Playboy *magazine.*

Sue: *Well, everybody likes to feel beautiful, but feeling beautiful can come from a sense of accomplishment. But we're told it's being 38-24-36 or something. Very few people are that.*

Betty: *Why is it particularly that beauty is related to women? Why must women be beautiful? You know, is this all we have?*

Sue: *It's all society says we should have.*

Betty: *Well, let's examine who society is. Who controls it? Who really is society?*

Phyllis: *When you look at business, who runs business —men. When you look at the church, who runs it—men. When you look at education, most of the teachers are women but who are the principals—men. When you look at any part of our society, labour unions, anything, anywhere—men. And so, when we say society, I really don't think we should hide behind this so much. We're afraid to say what we really mean, which is—men are the reason.*

Betty: *So, then what we are saying, in effect, is that men are the oppressors of women.*

Everyone: *Right. Right. Unanimously, right.*

Phyllis: *One of the things I think is so good about feminism is that we're ending competition between women. The mistress and the wife are in feminism together.*

Irene: *I think this is where we're really misunderstood. That we don't like other women.*

Phyllis: *You know, the first time I ever came to a meeting, I saw women in a different light. Before, when I was sitting on the subway, if I'd see a very heavily made-up woman with her hair all bouffant and dressed fit to kill to attract someone, I would look down on her. I would think, well, she's not in very good taste. And after just one meeting I looked at these women and suddenly I felt—not sorry for them—but this fantastic compassion, that we were really in this together. I felt a closeness with these people for the first time.*

Helene: *How many times in your life have you heard women say: "I don't like women." Of course we don't. We've been taught that.*

Betty: *But don't you think that because the male ego dominates the female ego that this makes it a political situation.*

Irene: *The female ego doesn't exist. There is no such thing.*

Sue: *Well, it's beginning to.*

Betty: *We're developing ego by the group.*

Sue: *What do you mean by ego?*

Betty: *I mean a sense of self. A sense of identity, of being a human being in this world. Not just a wife or just a mother, but a human being.*

Carol: *Yeah, even if you're rich. Or poor or whatever. You're just oppressed by being born a woman.*

Irene: *Right, we're all sisters. Prostitutes, call girls, strippers, factory workers. We're all sisters. We're all oppressed.*

Helene. *You know, a number of women ask why we don't let men come to our meetings. Well, my experience has been that generally if there's a man in the conversation, I've got to shut up.*

Carol: *Yah, it's in our heads. It's in our heads. It's up here and we have to play that role.*

Helene: *If a guy walked in right now, what would happen to all of us? We'd start playing our sex roles.*

Carol: *Even though we get past the point where we feel intimidated by men, it's still our revolution. They have nothing to do with it. It's our definition of ourselves. They'd just screw it up anyway. They're men. They can't be interested in us as women.*

Kathy: *Well, I'm new here and I like men. And I'm not going to cut them out of my life. Now, every damn thing you all have said is* true. *But still, I'm in this wavering stage. I've been oppressed by men, family, schools, dating, everything. But I'm not going to cut men out. I've got to live with them. They're there. And you all are just cutting them out.*

Helene: *I don't hate men. I just hate what they do. You can't just say I don't like men. I mean, who doesn't like them. It's just we don't like what they do. You know, some of my best friends are men.*

Betty: *You say you want good relationships with men?*

Kathy: *I want better relationships with everybody and that includes them, yes.*

Helene: *I've always tried to get honest relationships, but I haven't ever seen one.*

Phyllis: *I think we should see each other as human beings, not as one being superior or inferior. I would like my husband and I to be equals, I would even like to treat my children as equals and not be seen in a special role as policewoman or something. I want really good relationships with my family and the people I work with.*

Betty: *Oh, that's a mouthful of shit. It's never gonna happen and you bloody well know it. It's to a man's economic advantage to keep you down. He's not going to listen to you and say, yes, my dear, I want a good relationship too.*

Carol: *That's right. He doesn't give a shit. He wants to keep you down.*

Betty: *Saying, my darling, I want a good relationship with you. Don't you understand it's not going to work.*

Kathy: *Well, I see that these roles are hurting him too. That's why I want him to come around the way I'm coming around.*

Carol: *Do you think it hurts a guy because women beat up men?*

Betty: *How many men do you know get raped by women on the street? Do women go around raping men, if not in actuality, at least with their minds, with their eyes. Do they undress them as they walk along the street. Do they pinch men's bums?*

Helene: *Okay, there's something I want to ask about. I'm married. I have a family and I have said marriage is corrupt. Now how can I go on being a feminist if this is contradictory to what feminism dictates.*

Carol: *What do you think about alternative styles?*

Helene: *I've thought about what's the alternative. Well, a commune would be one. Or living alone. . . .*

Carol: *It always bothers me when people say, "Well, look at the alternatives. They're so bad, so can't you understand why I'm clinging to what I have." We have to experiment on our own as feminists. We have to get the hell out of here and try other things. You're saying that if you're about to leave you want to have a guarantee that there's something else you're going to be happier with.*

Helene: *I'm not about to go from a bearable situation to an unbearable one.*

Carol: *There's nothing worse than living with a male. There couldn't be anything more oppressive.*

Irene: *There's other things. There's living alone.*

Sue: *You'll find resources within yourself after having lived alone that you never knew you had.*

Betty: *Helene, what you're saying, in effect, is that the relationship between men and women under the present conditions should be salvaged, should be manipulated a little by women, but it should be maintained. But it can't be. Men are not going to accept it. They are going to fight it.*

Sue: *That's why we don't let them into our groups, right.*

Carol: *That would be bringing the enemy into our camp.*

Irene: *Why do we try so hard to patch things up with men. Why do we try so hard to stay living with a man.*

Sue: *Why don't men try to patch things up with us.*

Betty: *It's to their advantage not to.*

Carol: *This is exactly where the problem is—in our heads. We have to redefine ourselves. In a way we have to commit suicide as to what a women is and redefine it.*

Betty: *Why do we take for granted that there must be a male-female relationship?*

Irene: *Is sex with a man that important? Like we're taught it's the ultimate, the only sex—sex with men.*

Phyllis: *Well, obviously it isn't. I mean, when you realize that there is no such thing as vaginal orgasms then you realize it has nothing really to do with penetration by the male.*

Carol: *So it has nothing to do with the man, really.*

Phyllis: *We have to reexamine everything because so far it's all been written, researched, etc. by males. We have to start our own research. I think this is what feminism is about.*

Betty: *We not only have to redefine our own history, we also have to come up with a future for ourselves.*

Irene: *It's not going to happen in our lifetime.*

Betty: *This waiting for evolution is a lot of nonsense too.*

Phyllis: *I really think it involves a complete social revolution. Everything changes. And it's the next generation coming up that we as parents and examples are going to change. It's not going to be easy. Tomorrow, we're not going to find the alternative.*

Betty: *Well, how are you going to live feminism. If you are going to continue in a relationship of marriage, then what kind of an example is that to your daughters or to your sons. As far as I'm concerned I will couple-bust as much as possible. I think it's bad for a woman to even contemplate getting married. If I can discourage male-female relationships I will. I've done this in the past and I'm going to do it in the future.*

Carol: *If you want to share your life you can share it with a woman or a man.*

Irene: *Living with a woman today is a bad alternative, too. Because what tends to happen is that one of the women plays the female role and the other woman plays the male role.*

Carol: *It's the same problem, right.*

Phyllis: *When you're talking about women taking on the oppressor role like a male, this is if the women live together sexually. But like when we've talked about this at meetings, who do we really have the best relationship with, the really close emotional relationship? Who can you stay up all night and talk to till six in the morning and you really understand each other. It's the woman not the man. The point is, it doesn't have to be sexual. You can have a good friendship with someone without it being sexual. Then you don't have that male-female power thing.*

Betty: *Well, how do we do it. Do we organize our own armies, do we organize as a political party, do we go on sex strikes.*

Irene: *It's going to happen in many ways and we've got to accept all the ways it's going to happen. The totality of it will be a raising of consciousness of all people.*

Equal to What?

The first significant discovery we shall make as we racket along our female road to freedom is that men are not free, and they will seek to make this an argument why nobody should be free.

Germaine Greer
The Female Eunuch

We once had a conversation about women's liberation with a leading business executive. In the course of it we tried hurling our collection of economic and psychological grievances at him; these injustices, we argued, were a result of being born female. He retaliated with the statement that woman's work in the home is much more human and important than the business games he played every day.

Now, we had been to his home, and his wife served food and drink like a timid maid, saying hardly a word all evening. Yet his point is worth exploring. For here was a man who, although powerful, seemed confused and dissatisfied with his life. His case serves to point out why we do not seek to liberate women into the roles that men now play.

To pursue this point, we spoke to three different groups of men, asking them if they felt their wives were more oppressed than they were: a group of business executives, three working-class men, and three men whose wives are involved in the women's movement.

The executives believe that their wives are indeed freer in many ways than men. And as we interviewed them in their conference room in a large glass box of a building, we knew that we wouldn't trade places with them, even at their considerable salaries. They seemed sealed off from their own feelings and afraid of saying the wrong thing or losing face—or, as it emerges at the end of the conversation, of seeing themselves too clearly.

On the other hand, their position in the world held a certain fascination and appeal. As women we rarely have the chance to wield power directly. ("Dance," as they say in the westerns.) What does it feel like to be surrounded by secretaries running for coffee, trying to please, knowing that they are spending their small salaries on clothes to impress you? We wouldn't mind the chance, for a day, to see what it feels like. But that is an admission of a certain egotism that lives in us all.

We talked with the working-class men in the government housing project where they live. Two of them are unemployed, one because of illness. The third has a factory job. The willingness of these men to express themselves contrasts sharply with the executives' caution. Although they are in favour of equal pay for equal work for women, they feel most feminist ideas are valid only for middle-class women. Women who work in factories, they argue, are better off at home. They also share with the executives the view that children need their mother at home to give them a sense of security and moral values.

Many Women's Lib groups would consider themselves misinterpreted by the view that they speak only for middle-class women. While their position is that women must be aware of and fight their own oppression, they feel allied to other groups in fighting economic and political structures that hold both sexes down.

Women's liberation also sees the need for both parents to participate equally in raising children—an idea we wholeheartedly favour. But if the choice and number of jobs in the marketplace is severely limited, material survival will take precedence over demands for working hours that will allow men and women to share the duties and joys of childrearing.

The last group we spoke with was composed of three men whose wives are in the women's movement. An important part of the theory behind women's liberation is that it will help to liberate men, too, from role stereotypes and the burden of sole financial responsibility. All three, because of the nature of their jobs—one is in television, one on the faculty of a university, and one was, at the time, a supply teacher—have more flexibility in their lives than any of the other men interviewed. They feel that although it is often difficult to give up certain male privileges, they are pretty sure that they too are benefiting as a result of their wives' demands.

"Freedom is money," said one of the executives. But the management group is no closer to any kind of real freedom than the working-class men.

The Executives

Harry: *Do I think women are really worse off than men? On the contrary. I think it might be the other way around.*

Patrick: *If you take the ordinary man-woman, husband-wife relationship, I think that it's the man who's under certain pressures. He's tied to his job economically. He has a wife and family to support. He's not as mobile as he'd like to be. His wife, on the other hand, while tied to the home, is still free to make a decision to work part-time if she wishes, or to stay in bed, or to join a woman's league and play bridge. She is freer than the man. Finish your work in the morning, then you can read or sit quietly for a couple of hours. She can even go to the theatre in the afternoon. Those are luxuries I don't have any more.*

Harry: *I have five bosses. She has really only one. Me. And just for about three hours a day.*

Patrick: *I think one of the biggest misconceptions that women have generally is that we are fulfilled by our work. Actually, it's not true. While we might like our work and we have some flexibility, we are terribly, terribly caught up in the economic rush of making "x" number of dollars.*

Harry: *If I was a female, I think the only area of really great concern would be that my economic well-being and that of my children was tied to this individual that I've married. And if she's not a trained professional person she just can't go out and earn a living comparable to the economic level that he's supplying. And if a woman has the bad fortune to marry someone who's a ne'er-do-well, or who gets fired from the first five jobs he has, I would think that's a pretty serious threat to the woman.*

Patrick: *It may look like women are not as free as men, but really, when you make a decision at age twenty to get married and take on a career, you don't really know what you're doing. You're more or less pre-conditioned to feel you have to earn this living.*

Gabe: *I think that women get their priorities mixed up. Some women think that their husband, who has the capability of making $50,000 a year, is a more complete person or should feel more complete than she who is in the home. I think the job my wife does in the home is more important than the job I could ever do anywhere else.*

Patrick: *The fact of the matter is, irrespective of how much fulfillment you get from your job, somebody has bought you for at best nine hours a day, and generally, for most of us it's a lot more than a forty-hour week. Somebody has paid for your time and you've sold 33 1/3*

to 50 per cent of your life to fulfill this economic commitment you have.

Gabe: *I think we deal more with inanimate objects in business. We never really deal with real human aspects of things. Like, if you're dealing with children, it's a very human experience. But when you're dealing with some sort of product, you can't really get turned on by that.*

Patrick: *When she opts to have children, she has to be the focus for those children. When I was a kid, home was always there. I think my children need it and I guess I get a very comfortable feeling that my wife is at home looking after the children—and looking after me, too.*

Harry: *I don't want to be greeted at the door by a wife who says, "Do you know what Johnnie did today?" Children are her responsibility and it's wrong to extend them to her husband. Of course, you do want to hear about important decisions about the child.*

Gabe: *I think children are really much more important than you're making it seem. I don't know how many people have said to me that what they did during vacation was spend two weeks getting to know their kids. This is a great concern to a lot of men who are busy.*

Patrick: *I really don't have time to maintain some stability at home or concern or interest in my children.*

Gabe: *Why are we all so caught up with work?*

Patrick: *It's so constricting. You leave your home every morning and go into a tall box to work. My definition of liberated would be that my time was all my own.*

Harry: *Well, now, the work of a man is exciting in certain respects. It's exciting from the point of view of convincing other people to accept your ideas. Now that's really challenging and worthwhile.*

Gabe: *Here in North America there's an enormous economic crunch. Fulfillment is determined by how much money we make. There aren't many men who are fulfilled by the job they're doing.*

Harry: *Freedom is money. If you look at it, the rich guy is free. If you're rich you're free. That's obvious. Automatic freedom to do what you want. The reason we're here working is because we're not rich.*

Patrick: *I don't know. I think it's sort of a gradual thing. You wake up one morning and find yourself . . . you're not there, you know.*

The Working-Class Men

Peter: *You go into a factory all day long. You're filling orders. This is your job. It's the same old thing over and over again, day in and day out, week in and week out. After a while your mind begins to feel it. You begin to feel stagnant. You just feel like running.*

Phil: *Of course, often you realize that women on the same job are making much less money. That's something I've always resented.*

Peter: *There are so many angles. I remember a card factory once took about seven of us into the office and they told us, "Look, in this organization there's a possibility to become floor manager at $80 a week, and after that you could become a supervisor at $100 a week, and you could go right up to the Vice-Presidency at $27,000 a year." Now, a lot of those young guys with no education and not much work experience swallowed it hook, line and sinker. And so these young guys rip and tear their guts and break their necks. And it doesn't get them anywhere.*

Phil: *So what can the average guy do about his frustrations. You can't go to a gym. It costs money. You sure can't yell at the boss because you can only change jobs so many times. So what can you do to let go. Only take it out on your wife.*

Charles: *One of the problems with this women's liberation is that in the low-income bracket people have to work to live. If you're a woman in a professional field, you're in there because you like it. But here, the women are working because they have to work. I can't see where there's much pleasure in that. Working is forced on them by the high cost of living. And this is where women's liberation is going to have a very weak link in its chain. In the highest echelons of society a guy couldn't care less what his wife is doing—within limits, you know. He knows that she is quite capable of going out and earning a fairly reasonable living as an executive in a dozen different ways. We know our wives can't.*

Peter: *In my case, I was laid off due to sickness. And it's very difficult to be home and see your wife going off to work. But I strongly feel that if I'm home and not working, well, then certainly I have a duty to look after the house and the children and the meals.*

Phil: *I've talked to a lot of women whose families have broken up because the husband was unemployed. The women will tell you he was no damned good. Why? He wasn't working. You know, you really begin to feel that you're no good. You think, they'll be far better off if you walk out.*

Peter: *A guy gets up in the morning, say, looks out the window and sees somebody going to work. And he's been out looking for work himself. He's been out* looking for months. He's put in applications all over the place. He's been checking newspapers. Well, the next thing, he begins to wonder about himself. He begins to wonder if he's any value to his family. Is he of any value to society? He looks out that window and sees a guy going to work and says, what the hell. How come he can hold a job and I can't. What's the score here. There's 500,000 unemployed in Canada. There's men begging for jobs. And his wife begins to wonder. Does he really want to work? Is he really out there looking for a job?

Charles: *I don't think any man wants to see his wife going to work in the winter. I don't want my wife to work because I feel that her responsibility is in the home. When you stop and consider small children, I'm convinced that unless the hours a woman is working are such that she is at home when the children get home from school, it's a bad situation. I've seen that.*

Phil: *You know, it's the mother's responsibility, not only as a mother but as a human being—to give the children some guidance. They've got to try to give them some direction as to what they should be doing or what they should be looking for. Children are going to get their most basic instructions in love and care from their mother.*

Charles: *You talk about liberating women to work. What about the women down in Newfoundland, carrying the fish, fifty or sixty years old. I tell you, they have equal opportunities. If the man carries two kettles of fish she's got the same opportunity. She can carry two and if she can do better than that she can carry three or four.*

Phil: *If you're going to talk about liberation, how about liberating children from ignorance and giving them a start in school. We have women here who are qualified to instruct children in a "head-start"-type programme and can teach them their alphabet and how to read. Unfortunately, our women have to work to help support a family. There's a lot of money floating around in Canada. The city will call in a planner for a $75,000 job. He'll sit down and he'll plan for a couple of months, present it to council, the council will look at it and then it's into the waste basket with it. This money could be going to some of our women down here who'd love to get out of the factory. They love children. Why not give them a day-school and let them work with children.*

Peter: *When we say liberation, what we want is to liberate our children from the life to which they are doomed. The attitudes of teachers towards our children are nothing short of a disgrace to the democratic system. They tell children that there's no point in discussing anything. You'll never amount to anything, the same as your parents. Now, if we're talking about liberation let's liberate our children from this.*

Phil: *I would love to liberate me. So that I could devote a little time to myself. I'd like to sit down, try my hand at painting. I'd love to be able to express my feelings. Who's going to liberate me so I can do this. I would love to have time to read. In that sense, maybe my wife is a little freer than me.*

Charles: *I don't know what women's lib means by freedom. You know, there's freedom everywhere. You can be in the darkest dungeon and feel freedom. You sit down long enough, you know, and eventually you'll see beauty in many things.*

Peter: *They talk about freedom. Ninety-five per cent of women in the low-income group are working. They would love to be liberated from their jobs. They would love to get back into the home. What kind of liberation is working in a toy factory for $1.10 or $1.25 an hour, eight hours a day, with bosses standing over you? Is this the type of liberation you want? Or is it liberation to work in a field you want to work in?*

Phil: *Women are fighting for equal rights, and we're fighting, I tell you. We're fighting hard so that our sons have the freedom to go into any job they choose. Right now they're restricted by economics. Our girls too, certainly. Who's going to liberate our children?*

The Men in Women's Lib

John: *In the first place, we're not liberated. Almost nobody is now. Women's liberation is a liberating movement. That is, an attempt to move in a direction where there would be equality of opportunity, equality of work, different social attitudes in and out of the home.*

In our home we divide the housekeeping duties. I cook meals and wax floors. But I think the best thing about our eliminating the division of labour between men and women in the home is that I take part in the rearing of our child. He's not somebody that I just come home to at the end of the day. He's somebody that I try and develop with and understand and actually grow with. That's certainly very important to me.

Martin: *To be honest, I was really repelled by the idea of household duties. I was raised in a family where my mother did all the little things. She picked up after me. I didn't have to do anything, you know. And it's hard to get into the habit. Your wife normally picks up after you. But if she wants to get liberated, she's not so excited about doing those little things. We had a lot of fights. She'd say: "I'm not going to do that stuff any more. I go to work too. Don't give me any of that garbage. You have to sweep up once in a while." So we made a deal. She picked up in the house and I'd go out and do the laundry. Now, we have two kids, so there are five or six loads of laundry a week. So I went and did that in the snow and I felt it was helping. But she didn't think that was enough liberation. We added up the hours. I spent three hours out doing laundry and she spent six hours cleaning. Therefore, I had to do more cleaning. I mean, I see the point. I'm lazy and I'd rather not do it. But I love her so I do it and we don't have any more fights.*

Roy: *Happiness is relative. I remember when I was in high school having an extremely interesting discussion in our history class over the question of whether ignorance was bliss. And perhaps the slave owner was happier than the person who was in a more equitable relationship to the people who were working for him. But it's not a question of happiness. It's a question of fulfillment, as opposed to just existing for sixty-odd years on this earth. You're broadening yourself and opening up aspects of yourself that were denied you by your socialization.*

For instance, as a male I was socialized, as I think most men are, to be very competitive. And part of this competition is a certain emotional insensitivity, because when you're competing with someone you've got to be very hardnosed to your own emotions and insecurities. In the process you lose a lot of yourself. Your feelings are driven very deep inside you. Most men, for example, when they get angry, get physically angry. They feel like throwing their fists. They tighten up inside of themselves and maybe, eventually, let out a yell. And this inability to feel your anger and let it out just keeps building up. And certainly men can't let themselves cry. The opposite of this is that women are socialized to be more sensitive to feeling. And this is part of loving. The motherhood role is one of being open to your child and your own emotions. For a man that's very difficult.

John: *Since we've become aware of one another's lives and one another's problems, especially since I've become aware of the kind of problems she faces in raising a child and going to school and having a career, it's easier for us to confront our problems. We can talk much more openly and understand the situation the other one is in. There's a sense of us trying to solve a whole set of problems together rather than there being one kind of problem for me and another kind of problem for her.*

Roy: *You know, like men's image in ads. The man has this completely emotionless face, and he's tough and he's not showing anything from inside him on his face. He's a complete blank.*

John: *Now, the three of us have peculiar jobs. I think I end up putting in an eight-hour day five days a week, but I can shift my hours around. How many men are in my situation? No man who punches a time clock can do that.*

Roy: *I understand that in Sweden for two or three decades they've been making pretty serious efforts to equalize the relationships between men and women, and they've found out that in effect the eight-hour day is a conspiracy against equality. Because until a man starts doing housework and pulling his share of the load at home, cleaning up and going out and getting the groceries, he doesn't realize how much work there is.*

John: *Yes. What the movement has come up to is the realization that the kinds of issues that have to be fought are things like universally accessible and good day-care, equal job opportunities, equal wages for women, those kinds of things.*

Martin: *You know, one thing that's interesting is that you find people who you'd think would be against it and you find out how many people are really for it, in a mild way, of course. They're not going to have their wives going to meetings or marches and stuff, but they're open. I think a guy who is mature is not afraid of a woman having her own life, having other interests. And if your wife gets out and sees people besides the next-door neighbour, she can be a pretty interesting person.*

It's really freeing in the sense that I can look at my wife as a person, not as a sub-person who I have to take care of and look after. Being the breadwinner is

Isn't that what's-his-name in the Stetson?

Sure it is. But even if he weren't famous, he'd still look like somebody important. Because Stetsons do something for a man. Any man. Wherever he goes, whatever he does.

See the rugged new Stetsons at your dealer's now. Especially The Duke, with the crown you shape to suit yourself.

And remember, nobody ever looked like a nobody in a Stetson. (Photographs taken on location of "True Grit," a Hal Wallis Production for Paramount Pictures Corporation.)

Stetson Hats, Incorporated

quite a burden, and if you're with a liberated woman then you find you don't have that thing.

John: *For a woman to live through her husband is not only bad for the woman, but it puts a terrible burden on him.*

Roy: *I think that men who are hostile to women's lib feel threatened. At least in part sexually. When you laugh at people it's a nervous response. You used to laugh at black people and "Polacks". You laugh at groups that you think are sub-groups and below you because you're afraid to deal with them as equals, as real people. You can't conceive of women laughing at men. Men are serious. And what does seriousness mean? It means they're real.*

John: *For the average Canadian male it's not just that he doesn't want to give up what you'd call male privileges. It's this—that to earn a living for himself and for his family he holds down a job, perhaps a very hard one, that he works at all day. He might even have to moonlight. Possibly his wife works too. If she does, she probably earns slightly less than half of what he does —even for comparable jobs—so in that way his work has more importance to them. Well, he doesn't have the time or emotional energy to come home and start doing housework. He requires someone there to do that. Now, I think this is a tragedy—a trap that all of us are in right now. It's not a matter of his not wanting to give up this slave. It's a matter of not being able to.*

Roy: There are guys who think there's something wrong with a guy whose wife works and who shares the housework and everything. But that's usually a guy who's doing a job he doesn't really like. He's under an awful lot of pressure and under it all he really hates his job situation. And because he's out working nine to five he comes home and he's too bushed for any of this. He's really too tired to relate to his wife as a real human being. And his identity is so insecure that he couldn't handle any change in his present situation. So he justifies it by saying everybody should do what he's doing.

For him to get up every morning is tough. He comes home and tells his wife: "You don't know how hard it is to get up in the morning. You think I like working for C, G & L. No, I don't. Even though I'm making all this money. It's no fun. It's hard and it takes a man to do that." Then of course, he's going to want his wife to be supportive and say: "Oh, dear, I understand. You're under tremendous pressure and I love you very much. I'll take care of the kids. I know you're tired. I know that when you come home you are tense. I'll take care of it."

He's in a trap. It's not his fault.

In this chapter we have concentrated on some of the problems of men: the responsibilities they shoulder and the traps they find themselves in, whether it be the trap of poverty or of the success game. But there's no denying that at the end of the long line of put-downs there's usually a woman, soothing her man after his long day's exposure to the bruising world outside. So it is not surprising that men, in general, resist the ideas of the women's movement. What they have to gain seems to them abstract, what they have to lose concrete.

Postscript

The greatest hope we have for this book is that it will help bridge the gap between women and the women's movement, and contribute to removing the fallacious distinctions that segregate "women's libbers" from other women. While reading the book, we hope you experienced at least once a flash of recognition, a strong sense of identification with women speaking in these pages, that will form a link between you and the movement. We wanted the book to have the effect of a low-key consciousness-raising meeting. We wanted you to feel that you'd taken part in what we found to be the most meaningful aspect of belonging to the movement: the sharing of those experiences and emotions that once seemed unhappily your own problem (and worse, your own fault, resulting from your weakness), and the discovery of the common threads that link us all in greater understanding—in sisterhood.

That last word alienates many people. Calling another woman "sister" seems like some women's lib version of "comrade". What we mean by sisterhood is illustrated by our own experience in recording the interviews for this book, for the chapters on sexuality, motherhood and marriage. In this process we were not outsider journalists, observing from a remote position of "objectivity". We were "sisters", linked by so much common experience to the women with whom we spoke. What is perhaps even more significant, this book would never have been written, the two of us would probably never have been able to work together, without a little push from the concept of sisterhood. It allowed us to overcome our first reflexive attitude towards each other as women—the urge to compete.

We wish we could now draw a sweeping conclusion, pointing the way towards liberation, but we cannot. Once the myths of "femininity" are destroyed, woman assumes a new burden, that of freedom. Following through on self-discovery is not easy. The woman seeking liberation struggles against major obstacles both within herself and from others, including the key figures in her life—her husband, other men, her children, and parents. She cannot fall back on her old "feminine" crutches when dealing with a wholly new set of reactions from people.

For both of us the knowledge we have gained from women's liberation—from the time spent in the Toronto Women's Liberation Movement, from the women we have met, from the books we have read by all those who have laid the theoretical groundwork for the movement, from the experience of working on this book—has been illuminating, but it has also made our lives more difficult, more complicated. The new awareness has been compelling and fulfilling, but strenuous as well. It is not easy to accept the realization that we are truly on our own, dependent only on ourselves for identity and purpose—and that our friends, our families, our husbands, are people we share with and love, but no longer destructively depend on.